HOW TO COACH YOURSELF

Hi Trevor —

Hope all is well
for you and it
isn't too sunny/rainy
for the business!

Regards,

Mark June 2012

HOW TO COACH YOURSELF

ACTION • KNOWLEDGE • MINDSET

...SIMPLE STRATEGIES FOR SUCCESS IN LIFE AND WORK...

DR MARK J NUGENT

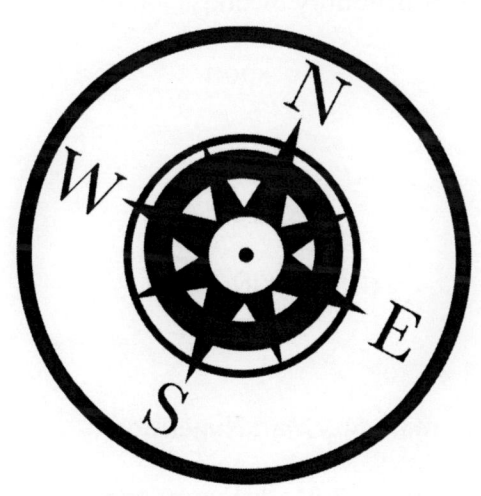

Published by:

Pure People Performance Ltd

BRC House

Bredbury Business Park

Stockport

Cheshire

SK6 2SN

UNITED KINGDOM

mark@DrMarkNugent.com

www.DrMarkNugent.com

ISBN: 978-0-9572497-1-4

Typeset in Calibri

I dedicate this book to everyone who truly understands that they and they alone are the captain of their ship.

This book is a collection of the best bits from my weekly blog Pearls of Leadership Wisdom.

My readers have been kind enough to make the comments you will see below. We all need feedback in this life and I am genuinely grateful to everyone who has taken the time to let me know that I have made a difference.

If you're looking for platitudes, generalities and 'feel-good magic bullets' - then you've found yourself in the WRONG place. If you're serious about your success, knowing you are the one who has to take control of your thoughts, your actions, your results...then you're definitely in the RIGHT place! Dr Mark - gives it to you and me - straight. No bull, no fluff, - just practical ideas, methods, systems, thoughts and actions guaranteed to make us more successful - whatever weird and wonderful definitions we may have of that emotive word success. Read on - you will be so pleased you did. **Peter Thomson - "The UK's Most Prolific Information Product Creator"**

I firmly believe that success is due to a combination of things and Mark covers all the bases: knowledge, action AND mindset. Every aspect necessary for success is covered here. **Gill Fielding - Founder Fielding Financial Family**

I have been reading Mark's Pearls of Wisdom since 2009. They are pithy, topical, funny and relevant. I would highly recommend this compilation as a useful reference for project , people and self - management whatever your particular business area. **Dr Nic Thompson - Process Technology Group Manager, Lonza**

Timely inspiration for daily and future success. **Clare Corran- CEO, Positive Futures North Liverpool**

The Monday morning Pearls is an excellent way to start the week. Just when I am planning what we are going to do in the office Mark's spark of inspiration arrives to help me along. **Graham Bowcock – Corporate Partner, Berrys**

Punchy, practical and humorous. Mark manages to highlight relevant issues or situations we can easily relate to then provides practical advice to take away and try for ourselves – all delivered in Mark's no nonsense style of writing mixed with humorous observations that regularly make me laugh out loud. **Jane Hayes- The Aspiron Group**

Although I have been in management for nearly forty years, I still look forward to my weekly "Pearl" from Mark. At this stage of my career I have usually heard it somewhere before in some form or other, but just to take the time out away from the daily chores and reflect on one aspect of your business or personal life is really useful in helping you focus on what is important. I also make sure I pass the weekly "Pearl" onto my children. **Andrew Ward- Marketing Manager, Greater Manchester Centre for Voluntary Organisations**

Palatable and incisive, Mark's blogs always resonate. Highly enjoyable and thought-provoking. **Joe Bell - Head of L&D, SCA Hygiene Products, UK & Ireland**

Mark's Pearls of Wisdom are a great way to keep you focused on your management style. I have been a Manager/Senior Manager/ Director most of my working life (40 years in management roles) but still enjoy the captivating way Mark portrays his messages and the Pearls Of Wisdom they continue to deliver. **David Kershaw - Director , CAE, FIMI**

In every great business book there are a few golden nuggets of invaluable information and advice. Without mixing too many metaphors, Pearls the Book is a collection of nuggets. **Ian Webster – Director, Achieve Limited**

Mark's Pearls always inspire me to take action that results in positive change. Whether that's changing mine - and others' - behaviour, rethinking our business strategy or the vital, daily reminder of the bigger picture, he's been a constant source of advice, reassurance and encouragement during my first year of running a new business. **Kate Whelan – Notch Communications**

Mark's philosophy is simple – work harder on yourself than you do on your business – and the Pearls are like a diet supplement to help you do so. **Karl Perry – Managing Director, Assured Events**

Mark's Pearls are an invaluable part of my working week. **Richard Dawson - Harlaco Webb**

Mark Nugent is the guy you want to help you gain clarity, focus and direction with your business. His experience, knowledge and know-how proved invaluable to me when I first took those tentative steps to self-employment. His pearls now keep me on track with advice and guidance and a smile. I have no hesitation in recommending Mark and his work. **Dave Verburg – Future-Focused Coaching**

Mark's "Pearls" are more valuable than simple wisdom – they are priceless common sense communicated with crystal clarity. **Amanda Fairclough FCA – Director, Amanda Fairclough Associates Limited**

Diving into Pearls is a great way of reflecting on and improving one's own performance. It has really transformed my thinking. **Mario Moustras**

Mark's Pearls, wild and cultured: they have a hard object and a soft centre – always an insightful read. **Michael Salmon – Director, Salmon, Heaton and Kimmins Ltd**

Pearls are, as the name suggests, small gems of insight that are quick and easy to digest, but more importantly are filled with straightforward advice that can be readily absorbed into your working practices. **Craig Valentine**

Contents

INTRODUCTION

In a nutshell this book is about simple strategies for success in life and work. Success - as *you* define it. No one else.

It was in late 2008 (I think it was October or November) that I wrote the first edition of a monthly newsletter for my coaching clients and friends. As the months rolled by and the second edition failed to appear, I realised I was not really in the monthly newsletter-writing business.

I needed to get my thoughts out in a pithier, punchier way. So, to satisfy this urge, in May 2009 I launched Pearls of Leadership Wisdom – a weekly blog on all things to do with managing ourselves and our opportunities intelligently and thoughtfully with the great hope of having a more fulfilling time while here on this planet.

This book contains selected posts from the Pearls blog. I have thrown some away with more than a little embarrassment. I have made some minor edits to a very few posts simply to aid clarity. In trying to make it all a bit more coherent, I have split the book into three parts.

Part 1 - Taking Massive Action - *Goals, Time Management, Personal Productivity and Brilliant Results*

Part 1 is all about taking large amounts of effective action. Being productive without burning out. I have put this section first because most of us can make huge strides in our personal productivity and get more and better results from our efforts. And, we can begin to do this today and get almost immediate benefits. That's why it's first.

Part 2 - What You Need To Know – *Strategy, Management, Leadership and People*

Part 2 is a collection of what I think we need to know to get along in organisations, even if we are alone in our organisation. So I've put together some simple, implementable advice on strategy, doing things properly, and getting along with others, whether they work for you or not.

Part 3 – Mastering Your Mindset – A User's Guide for Your Brain

When someone's talking about top sportspeople and they say "it's all about mindset at that level" everyone nods in agreement. Yet few of us wonder if it's also all about mindset in our lives and work. Well, *it is* all about mindset. Part 3 is the most important part of this book. When we understand how our mindset can assist us, how it can hinder us, and how to get more of the assist and less of the hinder, we can significantly increase the amount of our potential that we can realise. The sky really is the limit.

The ideas presented here come either from my own observations made during my corporate career and now with my clients, or they come from the work of others. I have tried to be diligent in my acknowledgement of the work of others but if I have made any omissions in this regard I am sorry.

My blog is written in a conversational style. This means my grammar is often...er...non-classical. I start sentences with *and* and *but*. I don't always include a verb. And as for the tenses... I beg your forgiveness.

Huge thanks go to Lisa Barnes (lisa@lsb-editing.com) for tireless proofreading, typesetting and great advice on publishing. More huge thanks go to Tom Broughton (contact@tombroughton.co.uk) for the cover design and the compass device. Work with these people if you can.

To all my subscribers – I thank you for your time, your comments and your interest.

Mark Nugent

PART 1

TAKING MASSIVE ACTION - GOALS, TIME MANAGEMENT, PERSONAL PRODUCTIVITY AND BRILLIANT RESULTS

It's a statement of the screamingly obvious but here goes – our results come from the actions we take. Perhaps expressed more usefully - great results come from taking a great deal of the right action.

Some call this *time management*. I don't like the term. It suggests that the issue is external to the individual – that it's about a thing...*time*. Really effective use of time, which I prefer to call *personal productivity*, is not about an external thing, it's about us managing ourselves – *self- management*.

In Part 1, there is a wealth of tools and techniques to help you become more productive. In particular my clients have found the idea of *high-payoff activities* to be extremely useful in focusing them on what actions to take.

You can triple you productivity overnight if you want to. Would that make a difference to you? It's all here.

THE TOP 7 REASONS FOR HAVING NO GOALS

Most people accept that having goals is better than not having goals. But then very few people actually have goals. Why the contradiction?

This is what people say:

I've got goals already!
I want to be slim, rich, travel to Australia, run the London marathon. These are not goals. They are dreams. Dreams are fine. A lot of goals start as dreams. But goals are different. They are written, precise, measurable, have an associated plan and a timescale for completion.

I don't know how to set goals
This is sadly believable because we are not taught how to do it at school. There's a process for generating and delivering goals. The process is not fool-proof. But life isn't a game of perfection. It's about stacking the odds in your favour.

I think I'll fail
Well, don't set a goal that you think you will fail to achieve. In order to be motivated we need to believe we have a pretty good chance of success. So set a goal you can achieve. But here's the good bit - in time, this repetition of success will embolden you and you will set more challenging goals until you are routinely achieving goals that would have seemed impossible a few years ago. And in any event, it is not setting high goals and failing to achieve them that is the world's problem, it is setting low goals and achieving them.

My friends will laugh at me when I tell them my goal
So don't tell them. And, in time, get new friends.

I don't need goals; I know what I'm doing
You do, to an extent. But you can stagger around in the fog, sort of heading in the right direction and you will, in the round, make progress. But having goals is like driving on a sunny day with clear

views and a map. You will also make progress, but an awful lot more of it.

I have goals...in my head.
See above.

Life is too unpredictable.
"Ladies and gentlemen, this is your captain speaking. We're going to take off and then make a right turn until the nose of the 747 is pointing directly at London. Then, we're going to relax for the next 7 hours. The cross winds, turbulence and general lack of order in our atmosphere means we may land anywhere from Reykjavik to Algiers. But hey, life's unpredictable. Thank you for flying with Unpredictable Airways."

Don't get me wrong. Sometime we have to simply react to external events. But let's not sacrifice all self-determination because occasionally life throws us a wobbler.

Goal setting starts are a chore, becomes a discipline, then a trusty tool. By that point you realise goal setting is the greatest skill you can learn. And the thing about skills is - you can learn them!

Success comes from goal-directed action.

Start small – have one goal. Set it now. What would you like to achieve by the end of this week that you would not have done if you had not read this blog post.

Do it now – take 2 minutes. You're worth it.

I was inspired to write on this topic by Brian Tracey **www.briantracey.com**. Despite sharing a surname, he isn't one of the Thunderbirds, but if that was his goal, he'd be one.

In a Nutshell...

> There are no good reasons for avoiding setting goals.

VISION

Some people really struggle with goals. They don't have any. This is not because they are worthless, feckless individuals. It's much worse than that. They are not guided by a vision.

I can see clearly now...
A vision inspires. A vision spawns goals. Goals with built-in motivation. And goal achievement is the definition of success. But a vision requires a leader. And leaders have vision. So we should be able to judge how many leaders there are by how many good visions we see...

Hen's teeth...
Frankly a good vision is hard to find; there are precious few of them around.

So how do you know when you have one?

- A great vision gives a worthwhile purpose to the organisation. Over the long term. It's your destiny.
- A great vision becomes the DNA of the organisation. All systems aligned in the execution of the vision.
- A great vision inspires. Inspiration is motivation's sexier sibling. We are helpless in its grip. It'll keep you up all night.
- A great vision challenges – no time for comfort zones here. A great vision should be a bit scary; a bit "can we really do that?"
- A great vision should be beautiful. And beauty cannot be hidden.
- A great vision is moral – absolutely. Global domination by force is a vision – a bad one. And you can be assured that others, with a superior, moral vision, will defeat the bad vision. We've done it before. And we'll do it again.

I am blessed...

Vision is the first stage in goal setting. And goal achievement is the definition of success. So if you have a vision that ticks all the boxes above – lucky you. You're living in a blessed world, where everything is just, well...better.

Eyes front...

If you are not so blessed, why not try to develop a great vision – this is leadership. It might be the most important thing you can do today. It might be the most important thing you can do, any day.

In a Nutshell...

A vision can and should be great and when it is it is your guiding light.

How To Achieve Challenging Goals

A few months ago I bought a road bike. I've never had one before. One of those funny bikes with bendy handlebars that droop down for no apparent reason. I've been riding a mountain bike for years now. Nothing too strenuous – a small 8 mile loop on soft ground three times a week. Helps me to clear my head...

But I felt I needed to do more so I bought the road bike on eBay. I set myself a big goal. 20 miles three times a week. Now the lycra-cladded amongst you will be snorting derisively. I know some of you are doing 120 miles in a single day. But I'm not there. For me, 20 miles seems like a lot. It's a big goal. I set the goal. I planned my route and off I went.

It was terrible...I managed it but it was exhausting. It seemed to take all day. And what are those stupid handlebars about? I thought I was going to die. The sweat was pouring off me and my head was pounding. And I knew everyone was looking at me, as I huffed and puffed my way around the Cheshire countryside. After what seemed like an eternity I finished the route. Twenty miles - in the bag.

Three days later I overcame all my fears and I did it again. A bit easier this time but it still seemed like torture. Mentally, I was pleased to have done it, but I was hardly left with a huge desire to repeat the experience, and in my heart I knew that doing this three times a week was not going to happen. I just could not picture it. As a consequence I was not motivated to try because it is near impossible to feel motivated to do something when you think you're going to fail.

I went back to the mountain bike. More my sort of thing.

Then the mountain bike had to have a repair and I was without it for over a week. Out came the road bike again. With huge trepidation. However, not being one to repeat past mistakes (usually) I started small – 10 miles. It took about forty minutes. It was fine. I did this three times a week for a fortnight. Despite the return of the repaired mountain bike I persevered with the road bike.

Then I upped it to 16 miles. Now I'm at 20 miles. I've just done four consecutive days at 20 miles per day and it was easy. Diary permitting, I can do 100 miles in a week. How long has it taken me to get to this giddy height? Nine weeks.

Now this is a major achievement for me.

My progress has involved starting small and building up. We all know this is the way to do things but for me it's been a stark reminder that to get anywhere we need to take the first step...

As Martin Luther King said, "you don't have to see the whole staircase, just take the first step."

The key to goal achievement is motivation and the key to motivation is a genuine belief that we will succeed. No self-delusion. A genuine feeling that in all likelihood we will succeed.

So...how to achieve challenging goals? Answer – set and achieve small goals. Take the first step...

In a Nutshell...
Huge goals can be overwhelming. Instead, set smaller goals. We need to feel we can achieve our goals if we are to take the first step.

GOAL SETTING

Our success is measured by the extent to which we reach our goals.

It's easy to write a goal, but effective goal setting is a wee bit more involved.

Does our goal tell us what to do **tomorrow**? If it doesn't we may never get started. So we need to develop smaller, sub-goals, e.g. 90 day goals.

Do we fully understand **what's in it for us** - all the benefits gained and losses avoided by achievement of our goal? This drives our motivation. Write them all down, by hand.

Have we considered the **barriers** that may block us? Working out how to **overcome** them beforehand makes us much more psychologically robust when barriers appear.

Have we considered the critical **actions** we need to do to achieve our goal and make sure that every day we do enough of them and do them first?

We must **track** our progress using a measure.

Developing an **affirmation** is beneficial: a positive statement in the present tense that we can believe, for example, **"I am a winner!"** We say this to ourselves every morning. We feel stupid at first, but it passes.

Visualisation – last Tuesday night on the radio I heard the footballer Wayne Rooney say "the day before a match I ask the kit man what strip we'll be wearing. Then I imagine scoring a goal wearing that strip, over and over, in my head". That's visualisation.

This is effective goal setting. And success is goal-directed action. So let's give ourselves the best chance of success. Aim high!

In a Nutshell...

Having goals is critically important but there's more to it than simply stating the goal.

AFFIRMATIONS

Rainy days and Mondays always get me down, as Karen Carpenter sang, after a holiday in Scotland no doubt.

We all have bad days. Days when we don't really feel like it. No energy. No confidence. Or we've just had a spat with our partner about a major issue of global import, like why don't you ever empty the dish washer I hate you aarrgghh...

That's where affirmations come in. An affirmation is a positive statement in the present tense that you believe. They say it's best to assume the goal has been achieved in the affirmation.

"I am the greatest." - Muhammad Ali. He said this before he was the greatest. When he was. And afterwards as well. It doesn't matter if it wasn't always true. What matters was he thought it was true. It worked for him.

Affirmations are a bit American...like believing in yourself, success and being a superpower. Don't knock it.

Why do affirmations work? There's a lot of stuff going on in our heads that limits us. It's probably a remnant from cave man and cave lady days when it was not a good idea to leave the cave unless you had to, for food or to find a mate, or get a club to deal with your existing mate. You didn't go for a walk on the savannah in 25,000BC for the sheer joy of experiencing a sunny day. No.

This stuff in our minds is called negative self-talk. "I cannot do this." "This is not for me." "Who am I to be able to aspire to this?" "I am not worthy."

Maybe some of it is put there by conditioning. By what you've been told. Over and over. Since you were a nipper. Who knows? But it's all a barrier. Most days we'll ignore it. But some days maybe it gets to us.

That's where affirmations come in. They replace the negative self-talk with positive self-talk.

So I had lots of affirmations. "I am financially free." "I weigh 12½ stone." "I have 75 customers." The problem with doing affirmations this way, where you imagine the desired goal as having been achieved, is that it doesn't ring true for me. I am not financially free (yet). I don't weigh 12½ stone (yet). I don't have 75 customers (yet).

I just couldn't believe the statements.

So I changed the way I wrote affirmations. I introduced the idea of being on a journey. Of being in the process of realising the goal. I am on my way to financial freedom. I am on my way to 12 stone. I am on my way to 75 customers.

This works for me.

So I say the affirmations every morning. And it's up to me to live up to them. To do what I need to do to make them come true. I am on my way to financial freedom. I can make that true by using the day to move a little closer to getting there. Or I can let the rainy day or Monday get me down. No chance.

I was inspired to write this by an email I received from Ted Nicholas, **www.tednicholas.com**. He's an American copyrighter and direct mail expert. His site is a bit cheesy, but that's just style. Don't let that stop you from extracting the huge value that resides therein, if you're interested in effective marketing.

Ted inspired me by sending me a copy of his affirmations. They are brilliant. Spot on.

No 8 is a cracker – "I cannot fail – only get results."

As is no 17 "I am what I learn."

Get them all here – **www.HowToCoachYourself.net**

Dr Mark J Nugent

I have stolen some of them and added them to my list because they ring true to me.

Thanks Ted.

In a Nutshell...
Giving yourself a regular pep-talk works wonders.

VISUALISATION

Visualisation is an important part of the goal setting process. It's like a television advert for your own future. And you are the director of the advert. But where it's different from a normal advert is that it creates the future. The advert isn't pulled from the programme. The programme is made from the advert.

Now, before you reach for the delete button, I am not advocating that you can think yourself rich, because you can't. No. You have to work really hard. But working really hard with the end in mind is much more effective work. And the end in mind, is the advert in your mind; the   visualisation.
When you have something to do that is important, and perhaps worrying, visualisation is a powerful tool to help you raise your game.

Lights, camera, action...!
I have a small talk to give today, in Macclesfield, and it's a bit different from any talk I've done before. I could furiously scribble notes down and try to memorise them, getting a bit stressed in the process. I used to do this, when I thought perfection was a good thing.

What I have done is this. I took a 3 x 5 inch index card and wrote down a few bullet points. No more than one for every two minutes of the talk. I then went and lay on my bed and I gave the talk, in my head, to an imaginary bunch of people in a place I've never been.

Can I do this in the car...?
No. Being relaxed is critical. Eyes shut. Lying down if possible.

How often...?
Depends on the event. I did this two consecutive times on Sunday morning and once this morning. That's enough. If I was addressing the nation on TV, I'd do it a bit more. But not much more.

What do I see?
I try to imagine small details as I talk. The faces looking at me. The ties. The necklaces. The temperature in the room. It's all made up. I've never been in the room. And I never will be truly in the room. I'll be in the advert for the room. The advert I've created in my head.

What do I feel?
Exactly what I want to. This is about setting the emotion for the talk. How am I going to feel – I choose how I want to feel and I put it in the advert – I chose to feel calm, clear, in control and on top of my game.

The advert is imbued by all of this...twice yesterday and once this morning. The job is done, before it's even begun. And will happen exactly as it has done in my head. The future is written, in my mind. The execution is a formality.

You can do this. Start with a small thing, something you know is going to happen, but you're not 100% confident about it. Then move on to bigger and bigger things. This stuff works...

In a Nutshell...
Repeated visualisation of a future event that goes well is a great way to make sure it really goes well. Top sports people have known this for ages.

REWARDS

A reward...
...reinforces behaviour. A reward causes the behaviour to be repeated, to increase in intensity. The reward does not need to be huge. It can be simple recognition. This is called positive reinforcement. The other side of positive reinforcement is when bad behaviour is also recognised with an appropriate level of chastisement.

In time, the good behaviour dominates. This is how we bring up kids (or should be) and it works on adults as well.

I've been a really good boy...
But something I think we do too little of is reward ourselves. Of course, achieving a goal will have lots of rewards associated with it, but sometimes they can be a long way off. An intermediate reward, say when you're a third of the way towards a goal, and then again when you're two thirds of the way there, can be hugely motivating.

Rewarding ourselves...
...has many psychological advantages. It facilitates learning and reinforces the behaviour required to continue. Plus it makes you feel good.

In a Nutshell...
Rewards have powerful, positive psychological effects yet are much underused.

ONE THING I DIDN'T TELL YOU ABOUT GOALS

The actions you take will determine whether or not you achieve your goals. So far; so staggeringly obvious.

But here's the thing...

What's your next goal..?

The one after the one you're working on now. What is it? You must have one. Spend some time on this.

The reason you need to define your **next goal** is because if you don't there's a good chance you will not achieve your **current goal.** You will not drive down a dead end street at 100mph.

And don't say you'll work out what the next goal is when you achieve the current goal. Because even if that were true, not knowing your next goal will slow you down dramatically. And, if and when you do achieve your current goal, you may find that you actually *are* in a dead end. A real one.

Level Up...
Goals operate on levels. Like quantum mechanics. There's generally considered to be only three levels. So it's easier than quantum mechanics. Relax.

Level 1 – Process Goals...
Think of process goals as inputs. That is, what you actually do. Also known as high-payoff activities (thanks to Paul Meyer at LMI Inc. for coining this phrase).

- I generate 7 "A class" prospects per week.

- I make 3 sales calls per week.

- I coach for 2 days per week.

- I produce and launch a product every quarter.

Level 2 – Performance Goals...
Think of performance goals as milestones on the road to a final destination. You still "do" them, but you are less directly in control of the result compared to a process goal.

- It is 31st December 2012 and my coaching and product sales are £X.

- It is 31st December 2013 and my coaching and product sales are £Y.

Level 3 – Outcome Goals...
Outcome goals are significant achievements or life events. The culmination of a lot of process and a lot of performance. The Level 3 goal is the next goal I've been talking about.

- It is 31st December and I have a business that covers my total life costs and produces a surplus of £Z and my commitment to this business is no more than 16 hours per week.

Here's what often happens...
You set a great goal at Level 2. The annual sales budget for example. You don't define Level 1 goals (high-payoff activities) so you reduce your ability to hit your Level 2 goal. I'm not going to bang on about that because this post is about the next bit...

There is no...
...Level 3 goal. There is no next goal. No context. No reason. No meaningful motivation other than stick motivation (as in carrot/stick). Because the carrot doesn't really work anymore. Either you've given up carrots or you have to take more and more carrots to get that great carrot effect. And the stick never worked at any level.

So there's no effective motivation left at Level 2.

Higher Ground...
The Level 3 goal, the next goal, is your purpose, your vision. The importance of purpose or vision is immense. In these pages of scribblings I have quoted wise words on this topic from both the Bible and The Clash:

"You better realise that you gotta have a purpose or this place is gonna knock you out, sooner or later."

"Where there is no vision, the people perish."

They're saying the same thing. You can guess the source of each quote.

Do this...
Spend some time getting a Level 3 goal. You may need to develop some more Level 2 goals to bridge the gap between your current goals and your Level 3 goals. Or you may be able to go straight to the Level 3 goal.

Whichever way works for you, do this and you will have tapped into the greatest source of sustainable motivation there is. And instead of modest goals being difficult to achieve, you will find that big goals become, if not easy, certainly well within your reach. Worth a try?

In a Nutshell...
If you specify the goal *after* your current goal, you will massively increase the chances of achieving your current goal.

EIGHT TIME MANAGEMENT DISASTERS

Time management remains a perennial issue for us all. There's too much to do and too much shiny stuff around that screams at us "look at me." There are a million characteristics of poor time management, but here are eight of the most egregious:

Having No Purpose
Yes indeed...the old purpose thing. What am I here for? Difficult to really get a hold of purpose but a good place to start is with values – what are my core beliefs? (beyond the stuff no one would argue with, e.g. fair, compassionate, respectful etc. etc.). What turns you on? What do you love doing? From purpose comes goals and from goals comes focus and from focus comes productivity – easy.

No real understanding of what's important
People make this mistake all the time. They have no real understanding of what will deliver success and what will merely facilitate it. Which is OK actually because it's not always clear, but it does need to be understood so if it's not clear, it's experiment time. Do stuff and if it works, keep doing it. If not, do something else. There are usually only a handful of critical activities that will deliver success. The rest are secondary and will not make the difference.

No self-improvement
What holds us back is usually inside us. We need to drag it out screaming into the light and drive a stake through its heart. It's a fight to the death and we must win. This is a time management issue because until we slay what holds us back we cannot be productive because you cannot be productive doing half the things you need to do – doesn't make sense.

No Assertiveness
You must have loads of this. With yourself and with all those around you. I trundled off with Jennifer and the boys to see a car today at a dealer who shall remain anonymous. The boys have a fixed idea of what they want – a blue convertible. It must be "blue, with a "wibbly-

wobbly roof". The dealer explained politely that this was a "90 minute process" – I assume he meant the sales process and not whatever it was he was doing with his hands in his pockets. That was his agenda. We had a different agenda – quick test drive of a specific car and then home for a chat (without the car salesman). There can only be one agenda – yours or someone else's. Best to make it yours.

No understanding of own rhythms
Not all hours are equal. Some of us are best in the morning, some are better in the afternoon. Different times of day are better for different activities. We can try to manage our diaries accordingly and do what's important when we are at our best.

Thinking multitasking works
Fragmenting our time into ever smaller slivers – ten minutes on this, twenty minutes on that. Total disaster. It is massively inefficient and is getting dangerously close to the fantasy that is multi-tasking. Our brains are much better with uninterrupted chunks of time on specific, single tasks.

Being Reactive
There's always a time to be reactive, but with some people it becomes the default. Almost all activity is in response to an external event – email, phone call, colleague's request – it goes on. Unless these people are offering to pay your mortgage this month, be very careful – they are trying to steal your time!

Having a To Do List
Oh no! Usually the number one symptom of many of the issues above...quickly throw it away, get out a big sheet of beautiful white paper and write on it the most important thing you can do now. Then go and do it. Once that's done....get out another sheet of beautiful white paper and write on it the most important thing you can do now. Then go and do it. Once that's done.......

In a Nutshell...

You cannot manage time, but you can manage yourself. Here's how.

TIME MANAGEMENT FOR DUMMIES

Write lists...
You must have lists. With everything on them – everything. Work through your lists constantly and try to score out more than you add on.

You must...
...become obsessed with your tasks. Get through the small stuff first, to clear the decks for the big stuff. Please those around you first: do what your boss/partner/child asks you to do. We need to get along with people. Answer the phone when it rings. If you're serious, get a nice leather binder with all the pages you need – diary, a page for phone numbers, London underground map, metric to imperial conversion charts, international dialling codes....

Well done! You've mastered time management for dummies.

Now...
Time management for smarties is different.

This is what to do...

Understand your goals. If you don't have goals, move quietly away from the computer and call me...NOW.

Once you have goals, then define your High-Payoff Activities (HPAs) – they are the critical actions that deliver your goals. Add two more - *planning and physical exercise*. You should have less than ten in total.

Half full...
When you plan your next week or fortnight, fill 50% of your time with HPAs (including meetings with yourself to do any HPAs that require no one else). Use your diary, or better, an electronic calendar like Office or Google (type calendar into Google).

For everything else, (emails, phone calls, actions collected throughout the day, actions collected in meetings, post etc.) process them all as follows:

Decide whether you will -

* Bin it,
* File it,
* Delegate it,
* Might do it one day, or
* Action it.

For the things that you may do one day, add them to a list entitled "Might Do It Today" Put this page in tomorrow's slot in a bring-forward file (a concertina folder with 31 slots marked 1 to 31 for each day of the present month and a second concertina folder with 12 slots marked January through December for the months we're not in at the moment).

If you must...
For those that you must action, and only those, do the following:

* If it will take less than 2 minutes, do it now.
* If it will take 2 – 15 minutes, put "the action" (hardcopy email, handwritten note etc.) in your bring-forward file to do it on a specific day (just before it must be done, no sooner). File all associated stuff (email, notes etc.) or bin them. Don't leave anything in piles, in your inbox etc.
* If it will take more than 15+ minutes to do it, schedule time for it in your diary and put "the action" (hardcopy email, handwritten note etc.) in your bring-forward file to do it on a specific day (just before it must be done – again, no sooner). File all associated stuff (email, notes etc.) or bin them. Again, don't leave anything in piles, in your inbox etc.

THE MOMENT I WAKE UP...

At the start of every day, look at your diary (week to a view) and your bring-forward file. Your diary is your plan. Remember, if you don't have a plan, you are part of someone else's plan. And do you know what they have planned for you? Nothing much.

Your bring-forward file for the present day will contain the trivia that you MUST do, and your "Might Do It Today" page of things you may do one day, or may never do, but don't want to forget about. Each day, you will look at this list and you may decide to elevate one or more of the items to actions which you will then process as above. Once you have done this, put the "Might Do It Today" list back in the bring-forward file under tomorrow's date.

Do you have piles...?
The great thing about this approach is it gives you clarity and focus. The HPAs get done. They are your number one priority. There are no piles on your desk; no piles in your inbox; no piles in your head and no bits of paper everywhere that cause a general sense of malaise.

In this system, everything has been processed and if it merits your time it will be in your diary or your bring-forward file.

This system is not just for work, it's for life.

Twinkle, twinkle...
Do this for a month. Then increase the time spent on HPAs to 60%. Do this for a month. Then 70%. That's probably as far as you can go, but by then you will be spending almost 5 times as much time as most people on your HPAs. You will feel in control, on your front foot, more confident and you will achieve more and more. It's a virtuous cycle. You have become a star player!

In a Nutshell...

Most time management approached are businesses built on a "consumables" model – you have to buy new "bits" every year to keep using them, like this year's diary. You don't need this. You need to know what's important, focus on that and squeeze everything else into an ever smaller box. This is true personal productivity.

HIGH PAYOFF ACTIVITIES

The secret to success is goal setting followed by ACTION. But what actions to take? The critical actions we need to take are called High-Payoff Activities because they propel us towards our goals.

So everyone spends all their time on all their High Payoff Activities?

What's the problem?
Well, there are two problems:

Firstly, we see that people spend too little time on their High Payoff Activities. Usually, only 20% of their time as a maximum. This is like an engine that only works for two hours per day.

Secondly, we see that people do only some of their High-Payoff Activities - they avoid those they do not like. This is like an engine firing on only two out of four cylinders.

So we see engines running for two hours per day on two cylinders instead of running all day on all cylinders.

The difference over even a short period of time is profound.

The first problem is about personal productivity and the second is about what holds us back.

Get this right and you've cracked personal productivity.

In a Nutshell...
Most of us are extremely unproductive.

How To Define High-Payoff Activities

I tend to bang on endlessly about **High Payoff Activities (HPAs)**: the things you need to do to achieve your goals. And if you do not do them, you won't achieve your goals. HPAs are not facilitatory or merely helpful; they are the critical, core, essential activities without which goals will not be achieved.

Define these, and spend 50% of your working day on them, and you will do very well thank you very much.

Some people ask me how to define HPAs. I have to admit to being surprised by this question, but I've been asked it so many times now that clearly it needs to be addressed.

If you really don't know where to start, ask your boss. Or find someone who's done what you are trying to do (a mentor). Or someone who can help you reach your potential (a coach). These people can be real and sitting in front of you, or you can find them in books, on courses, on the internet.

But let me give you an example from my life. It helps to start with a goal. So here's a goal:

I will generate £X profit this financial year.

Simple and necessary. I have bills and two cost centres to look after.

So, how am I going to achieve this goal? That's the HPAs. Goals are outputs, endpoints. HPAs are activities.

Because I understand my business, I know that to make £X I need to work with 20 clients. I'll get about 5 through repeat sales, i.e. they will phone me. So now I need 15. I need to prospect. So here's some prospecting HPAs –

HPA1 Continue to write my blog (one post per week).

HPA2 Go networking (once per week).

HPA3 Conduct an email marketing experiment with purchased data (by end July).

HPA4 Market a one day workshop every 6 to 8 weeks (ongoing).

HPA5 Implement a list building strategy generating x sign-ups per month (by Feb).

These HPAs will generate sales opportunities so I have another HPA—

HPA6 Sell and win coaching work (measure conversion rate of prospects to clients; track average client profitability) (as required).

And this of course produces another HPA –

HPA7 Delivery of coaching service to clients (as required).

Then there's an HPA all of us should have -

HPA8 Plan and Review (quarterly, monthly, weekly).

An HPA must have a measure associated with it. "Go networking" is insufficient. "Go networking once per week" is better. "Go networking once per week and generate one lead per week is even better." I could take that further.

Eight HPAs. That's it. HPAs 1 to 5 generate leads. If they generate insufficient leads for the effort involved, I will change them or scrap them.

All of these leads, with a known conversion rate and a running calculation of average profitability per client will tell me with a good deal of certainty if I am going to achieve my goal.

There are other things I could do that might facilitate goal achievement – have a spectacular website, write numerous marketing pamphlets, hone my services until they shine etc. – but are they essential, core and critical? I don't think so but there's a bit of judgement required here between what's an essential HPA, and what's merely facilitatory.

Do the essential first and if you have some time over, do more of the essential – never get to the facilitatory.

Spend 50% of your time on HPAs – all of them mind, not just the ones you like. How much time you spend on each is a judgement call. HPA8 is your satnav and will correct you as you go along.

A small subtlety about HPAs – they need to be done. But not necessarily by you. If you have an HPA you are not skilful or confident about, delegate it or outsource it. If you cannot do that; get skilful, then competent, then confident. An unaddressed HPA will severely limit your chances of success. Be honest with yourself.

HPA8 is critical – planning and reviewing. Take time out every quarter to look at purpose and direction (strategy). Every month to make sure the short term (6 to 12 months) is on track. Every week to manage the forthcoming week and make sure you're at 50% productivity.

In a Nutshell… Identify your high-payoff activities and do them and you will be very successful. Simple.

Personal Productivity – Part I

It is true that time is the only commodity that we cannot buy more of. And we all have the same amount. And those who earn twice what we do don't spend twice as long earning it.

I have mentioned **High-Payoff Activities** - the things we do to deliver our goals. **Personal Productivity** is about spending as much time as possible on these activities to the aggressive exclusion of everything else. Most people spend no more than 20% of their time on **High Payoff Activities**. We can increase this to 60 - 70%. Imagine what that does to our goal achievement and hence our success.

The writer Stephen Covey talks of **Big Rocks**. You can fill a bucket with Big Rocks, then gravel, then sand, then water. In that order. Try doing it the other way around. The **Big Rocks** are our **High-Payoff Activities** - the actions that will directly determine how successful we are. The gravel, sand and water are the little things that don't matter. They are **Low Payoff Activities**.

Knowing what our goals are and what **High-Payoff Activities** will deliver our goals, we look at our calendar and we check that we have put the Big Rocks in the bucket first: today, tomorrow and every day.

In a Nutshell...
You have three priorities and High-Payoff Activities are numbers one, two and three.

Personal Productivity - Part II

"You must do the things you think you cannot do." - Eleanor Roosevelt

We have spoken about getting our High-Payoff Activities done first – getting these Big Rocks in the bucket first – before the gravel, sand and water.

But there's a subtlety
We may have four or five High-Payoff Activities that deliver our goals. Maybe we do lots of number one and two because we like doing them. Then we do a bit less of number three because we're not so keen on it. We do very little of number four. And as for number five – we really don't like doing that, we feel uncomfortable doing it and we're convinced we're no good at it anyway.

If we fill our bucket with only half the things we need to do we have chosen to limit our potential. Our engine is running all the time which is good but we're firing on two cylinders instead of four.

And what is it really about the things we don't like. Will they kill us? Will they humiliate us? Are they really so bad? Or is it just that we're not comfortable? We feel a bit of discomfort so we stay in our comfort zone? Because it's easy.

Well here's a thing – if we stray outside our comfort zone our comfort zone catches us up. It comes after us and envelopes us and we are back in our comfort zone but it's bigger and we are now doing all the things we have to do to be as successful as we want to be.

The key is action. As an example, if we hate making telephone calls we should make five every day and do them first thing in the morning. Regular and often. Regular and often. Frequency and repetition are critical.

Brian Tracey tells us that if we have to eat a frog, we do it first thing. Don't procrastinate. At best we'll eat the frog last thing and then all that's happened is that we've fretted all day. At worst we don't eat the frog and go home, defeated. And tomorrow the frog's still there, on our desk, sitting beside a new frog. Now we have two frogs to eat.

Little and often is habit forming. In time, days and weeks not months, we will have new habits, a bigger comfort zone, less fear and more success.

Eat the frog!

In a Nutshell...
All our High-Payoff Activities must be done, not just the ones we like.

BE A BLOCKHEAD

It's amazing when you first become self-employed. There's lots of time. The days are long. This is not because you have nothing to do. It is because you have no trivia to do. The trivia has not had a chance to build up. All the emails, voicemails, post-it notes and things on lists.

I got a sneak peek into this some years ago. I had been out of the office for a month. Yes, a month. I had something to do. I did not look at email. I made no phone calls. No one was to contact me unless there was an off-the-scale emergency that ONLY I could deal with (difficult to imagine what that might be).

No one called.

Having done what I had to do, I was travelling home by boat. I was looking out of the porthole in my cabin as the vessel pulled out of the dock and I realised my mind was blank. Not blank = stupid. But blank = blank sheet of paper. There was no noise. No lists. No squawking. No "can you just...?" No "have you got a minute?" The trivia had melted away. I had been working for 15-odd years and I had never experienced this before.

I was in a block of pure, clear time. I had no worries or concerns of any kind. No pressures. I was amazed at how slowly time moves when there's no noise.

There are two massive benefits to being in a block of uninterrupted time.

The first benefit is obvious. A big block of time allows us to focus all our energy on the significant issues that face us. And how well we deal with these significant issues will pretty much define what we get out of life. Think of this as the **chance** to score a goal.

The second benefit is maybe not so obvious. The distracted mind is much less able than the clear mind to convert **chances** into **goals**. And the piles of trivia that build up, even if we push them to the side during the blocks of time we schedule for the important stuff, steal some of our brain's bandwidth, because you cannot truly put them out of your mind.

You know what it's like when your PC slows down because you've got too many applications open. The majority of the applications are not consuming much CPU time but their very existence requires your PC to commit some resources to them and as a consequence there is much less capacity for the important stuff. And when a chance to score a goal arises, you kick the ball over the bar. Because you were thinking about something else.

So what we need to do to score more goals is to:

a) Create lots of chances *and*

b) Turn them into goals more often

We can create more chances by scheduling as much of our time as possible into big blocks (at least 3 hours) to work on the big stuff.

Second, we can convert more of our chances into goals by minimising distraction. The best way to do this is to throw all this rubbish into a bucket, or write it all down on a piece of paper and only give it attention once a day, for as short a time as possible. I'd say one hour per day. In this time, deal with all your email, all your phone calls, all your post – everything. In an hour. You may need more, depending on the nature of your job, but don't give this task more time than it truly merits. Give it what it merits, not what it wants.

And accept that after the hour or so is up, there may be some of it left undone. That's OK.

There is no point in being ready to score if you never get a chance – so schedule the blocks of time to create the chances. There is no point in creating loads of chances if your neck-top PC is so pre-occupied with trivia that you cannot score.

I may never again attain the fabulous blankness I had on that shiny day in that boat, but there are lots I can do to get pretty close, and stick that ball in the back of the net.

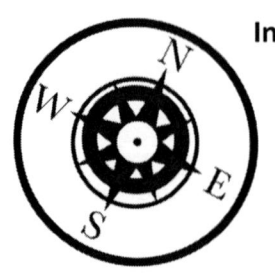

In a Nutshell...
We are at our most effective and efficient when we can dedicate big blocks of time to a single task.

How To Get More Done – Don't Multitask

I aim to be 50% productive and usually manage it, (15% being the norm). What I mean by that is I aim to spend 50% of my time on high-payoff activities – the activities which, if neglected, will lead to goal failure. Most people are around 15% productive. Strange but true.

I spent all of last Friday doing one particular high-payoff activity. A single task. I scheduled a full day for it in my diary. It involved me teaching myself something I needed to learn. I had no distractions - no email, no phone calls...nothing. I completed the task – I learned what I had to learn. I switched the phone and email back on at 4.30pm, dealt with what could not wait and then switched everything off again, all before 5.30pm.

I felt wonderful. In control, purposeful, satisfied. It was a good day in the office.

It reminded me of the critical importance of focus to productivity. Focusing on one task for an extended period of time. At least half a day. It feels like a luxury, but it isn't. A whole day is even better. With the phone and the email turned off. Check them every two hours if you must. But don't get sucked in – just check them and only deal with what is truly urgent. And that means urgent to you, not the other person.

In any working week, it is much better to give each of ten high-payoff activities a half day than to spend each of the five days doing all ten high-payoff activities for 45 minutes each. That's the road to madness.

This is because our brains work at their best when we allow ourselves to focus. Multi-tasking only works at a trivial level – I can drink beer, eat pizza and watch the football at the same time but these are not high-payoff activities. You cannot do two high-payoff activities at the same time. I've said this before but it's critically important that we reserve substantial chunks of time for the important stuff. Our world has a huge and increasing ability to fragment our attention to the point where we are so distracted we cannot function properly.

So when you catch yourself doing a dozen different things in a day and rushing around like a mad thing, it's time to ask if you're really focused on the important stuff, or have you slipped into "I must get through my to-do list" mode. You cannot get through a to-do list. It's against the laws of physics.

As I keep saying to my clients, chief execs don't stand up at the annual general meeting and say "we had 98% to-do list completion last year". No. They talk about metrics that represent goal achievement...sales, profit etc.

Here's another wee prompt – when you hear yourself say "I'm busy" remember that "busy" is usually a euphemism for "I don't really feel in control". And you cannot achieve when you're not in control.

You can achieve when you identify your high-payoff activities and give them the time and space they deserve. And you will become calmer, clearer-headed and you will get what you want.

Strange as it may seem, you can get more done by focusing on what needs to be done.

In a Nutshell...

Multitasking doesn't work for the important things.

FOCUS

Success comes from goal-directed action. Period. You need to focus on your goals. Because you get what you work for. Because you are what you do repeatedly. This requires focus.

Your brain craves focus...
Multitasking doesn't exist at any level other than the trivial. I don't know what your critical goal-delivering activities are. Mine are writing, prospecting, selling and delivery of my services. If you can do these at the same time I've got a high paid job for you.

If you don't focus on your goals...
... your brain will focus on trivia. Like the to-do list that never ends with all the little bits of banality that make up life. What a life – hey, I spent 40 years clearing my to-do list...and failed

.

The two minute test...
Here's what to do with trivia – if you cannot delegate it and MUST do it, and you can do it in two minutes, then do it. We are not robots and the little satisfactions we get from completing the small stuff are good for us. But for the rest of the trivia - write a to-do list by all means, and then file it. Every day, look at it. When something on it has festered so much that you MUST act – then act. Otherwise – put it back in your file until tomorrow.

Please please me...
Don't please other people for that reason alone. That's just conditioning. Please yourself first and you will find that you do please others – your customers, your partner, your bank manager. Concentrate on High Payoff Activities – the critical actions that will deliver your goals, your potential and your future. Getting through your to-do list is not a life goal, if you have life goals.
And you should.

It's all too much...

Some people only have big goals and that's great. But they can still be unfocussed because their capacity to deliver is less than their capacity to invent goals. They have too many big goals. Let's grow two businesses at once – wrong.

Get proficient...

...at goal setting, goal achievement, identifying your high payoff activities, dealing with your barriers, correcting any faulty thinking, developing confidence and eliminating procrastination. Until then, one big goal and a small handful of little goals are quite enough for anyone.

You can only do so much.

Protect your time like it's the most valuable thing you own, because it is.

You are what you repeatedly do.

You get what you deserve, not what you need.

In a Nutshell...

Most of us are not focused enough most of the time. This leads to the results most of us get – average results.

WHY IS TIME MANAGEMENT SO EASY FOR THIS GUY?

There's this guy I know. I've known him for about 8 years. He can be a bit immature sometimes. But most of the time he's really impressive.

He finds time management, or personal productivity, really easy. For him it is not a discipline, or a chore, or any such hard work.

He just flows. He is effortlessly focused on doing his high-payoff activities – the key activities that will deliver his goals. He relishes them. He can spend hour upon hour on them and he never gets tired because he's in the zone...that place where what you do is not hard work, it's living...like playing the guitar, or driving a racing car, or whatever it is you can do that requires a lot of skill but for you is easy, almost effortless.

He suffers no distraction.
He does not eat when in the zone. It's not that he chooses not to. It just doesn't cross his mind. There are one or two HPAs he is not comfortable doing, so he delegates them without hesitation and does so effectively. He makes it clear what he wants and when he wants it done (usually now) and he does not tell those to whom he delegates how to do whatever it is – he is only interested in the result.

All the small stuff sent to drag him off track is as nothing to this guy. He simply doesn't see it. I was talking to someone the other day and they told me that sometimes when they speak to him he seems not to hear them. He doesn't react. Or rather, he doesn't react to them. This person told me, in all seriousness, that he thought the guy might be hard-of-hearing.

He's not hard-of-hearing.

He doesn't get distracted by email. The first email I ever sent him – it took him eight weeks to respond to me. Eight weeks. With a six word answer. Doesn't he know who I am?

How does he do this?
How is it that for him, time management is not a chore, it's the default? For him, dealing with all the nonsense in life is the chore. He is focused on the goal, knows what needs to be done, works like a demon, delegates like a machine, doesn't sweat the small stuff and gets exactly what he wants, on time and in full.

For him it's easy – he has a purpose statement. He blurted it out to me the other day. Well, in pieces, over the course of the day. It wasn't well formed in his mind but because his purpose is so meaningful to him, wasting time on anything else isn't an option. His purpose drives him, satisfies him completely. So why would he willingly spend any time on anything that didn't serve the purpose?

I cannot tell you his purpose...
...but the form of it goes like this –

"The purpose of my life is to be......(put adjectives and nouns here),

and to......(put verbs and nouns here),

so that......(put the outcome you want here).

Here's a (boring I'm sure, I'm just about to make it up) example –

"The purpose of my life is to be a diligent, attentive and effective teacher, and to practice and perfect my teaching skills, so that I am most able to help others to develop themselves and have a more fulfilling life."

In fact it's not so boring when I look at it.

Now if the idea of a life purpose freaks you...
...make it for the next 30 days. Or a year.

Today, this guy I've been talking about has such a purpose. I expect his will change and be different next year. But today, he has it, pure and true, and that's why, for him, being effective is a walk in the park.

Dr Mark J Nugent

He's only 8 years old, as you've guessed, but he's great. And I'm not saying that just because I'm his Dad. It's part of my purpose to help him stay on his purpose, whatever he defines it to be, because then he'll find things a damn site easier, and a lot more fun.

In a Nutshell...
Purpose is the best, maybe the only source of lasting motivation.

Everything You Need for Your Best Ever Year is Here

When I put my annual plan together for the forthcoming year, I've realised that I used quite a few tools, techniques and mental skills that not everyone is confident in using. And yet more of these tools, techniques and mental skills will be required to make it all happen over the next twelve months. So I've put them all here, in one simple to digest, tasty blog post.

There's twelve in total. Let's call them **levers** because a lever is something that allows you to focus your effort in a very efficient way with little or no wastage and this is what all twelve will do for you.

You may not need all the levers. But all the levers you need are here. I reckon you can learn how to use one in a week. That means you can make all of them a part of who you are and what you do by Easter.

This is it. We are in the second half of January already. Now is the time. You have nothing to lose. Nothing.

I have suggested the order in which you approach each lever, but it's just a suggestion.

So here's goes...

Lever 1 – Get a Purpose
Why? – Purpose is the source of all motivation. Without it you have no purpose. Obvious really.

Lever 2 – Set Great Goals
Why? – If you don't know by now...

Lever 3 – Triple Your Productivity
Why? – despite the arrival of the internet, and imbecilic books like the Four Hour Work Week, winners still work like dogs. Same as it ever was. Talent is not enough.

Lever 4 – Do What You Hate
Why? – Because if you procrastinate on important stuff you are destined for mediocrity. Sorry about that.

Lever 5 – Manage Distraction
Why? – Because if you don't you will be distracted and then where will you be?

Lever 6 – Be Present
Why? – You cannot do your best if you are not here, in the room, paying attention.

Lever 7 – Know Who You Are
Why? – If what you want to do, be or get is not part of your identity, it either won't happen or it won't last. (See lottery winners).

Lever 8 – Be Assertive
Why? – It's what adults do. (The alternatives to assertiveness are what children do. They are safe for children but toxic when done by adults).

Lever 9 – Manage Your Emotions
Why? – If you don't they will manage you, and people will think you are undeveloped, because you are.

Lever 10 – Be Self-Efficacious
Why? – Because if you're not your feet will stick to the ground.

Lever 11 – Be Resilient
Why? – Because you will get results you don't want and how you react to that matters...a lot lot lot.

Lever 12 – Conquer Fear
Why? – The perennial slayer of human potential...draw your sword for a fight to the death.

That's it – and you can find it all in this book.

Rock solid good stuff that works every day of the week and has been the foundation of greatness since the earth's crust solidified. It's not easy but neither is it difficult.

So, if you haven't already, sell your TV on eBay, give up the booze two days a week as the government recommends and put an hour in your diary every Monday to study one of the levers and put it into practice.

In twelve weeks, you will be a very happy bunny.

In a Nutshell...
We have everything we need to achieve everything we want.

THE GREATEST QUESTION TO ASK YOURSELF RIGHT NOW

When you're going about your job, and you are wondering what to do next, there's only really one question to ask yourself:

What's the most important thing I can do NOW to move closer to my goals?
Now if you've been in my presence for more than two minutes you will have a list of high-payoff activities – the critical activities which will deliver your goals and if you ignore even one of them, or fail to spend enough time on all of them, you WILL NOT achieve your goals.

So go to the list and scan it and choose the most important one and do it next. Repeat to fade.

Some people don't like filling their diary with high-payoff activities. They like a bit more "freedom". I hesitate to say it but that's actually all right, provided the lack of diary-planning isn't a productivity avoidance technique, but only you will know the answer to that.

I have one client who hardly ever uses her diary at all – but she has a list of high-payoff activities and when she's spent a couple of hours on one she moves onto another. She's very productive without actually scheduling anything. She's disciplined. She doesn't let the lack of a schedule turn into a lack of productivity.

One of the great things about this question - **What's the most important thing I can do NOW to move closer to my goals?**, is that you cannot seriously answer "clear my email", "do yet another edit on that PowerPoint", or any of the other myriad issues that push and jostle their way into our field of view.

Here's an idea – write the question out on a Post-It note and stick it on your screen, close Outlook, switch off your phone and spend the next two hours taking a giant stride toward your goals. Bliss.

In a Nutshell...

This is a great question. Stick it to your monitor. The answer is not "do my email."

WHO'S STEALING YOUR ENERGY?

The energy you have to spend on what you want to do today and in the future is the total energy you generate minus the amount that's lost to the dreaded energy suckers.

Let's start on the supply side...

You do generate energy, quite literally. Of course we are not aware of this happening so we don't think of it that way. But it's true. Most of us have more energy than we need. It just doesn't always feel that way.

Let's look at the demand side...

Like some massive octopus in a schlock sci-fi film, energy attracts suckers. Energy suckers swarm all around you in a feeding frenzy and they will leave you with nothing if they can.

The energy suckers take many forms.

Here are just some of them -

1. Bad Environment
Too noisy, too hot, too cold, too light, too dark, bad feng shui (don't laugh – who likes sitting with their back to the door?)

I once had a client who said of one of her charges "she's easily distracted". She worked in an entirely open plan office with no baffles and 75 people standing up doing telesales. Easily distracted! She'd need to be comatose not to be distracted.

Get your "area" sorted.

2. Bad Relationships
Continuing to deal with people who don't play the game fairly: who are aggressive, passive-aggressive or passive. People who don't have their Mum in the office, so they use you as a surrogate. People who

wish to cast you as a major player in whatever mini-psycho drama consumes them this week.

The greatest things you will come across in this life are people, but not all of them. Some, I'm afraid, do not live up to the billing.

Kiss them good bye.

3. Bad Self-Management
Big no-no. From pretending you have goals to only doing what you like; the list of possible self-management failures is long, long, long. Doing the same thing over and over again and expecting a different result – madness as Einstein said. Fearing failure whilst understanding that fear of failure guarantees failure.

As Steve Jobs said (before he knew of his final illness) – "we are all going to die, so what is it you're scared of losing?"

Manage thyself!

4. Bad Management
Not treating management as a skill to be learned (the real British disease).

I used to do chemistry. I'd make molecules. Sometimes I'd turn A into B into C into D....all the way to L (I think the longest piece of synthesis I did was 12 steps). If you do each step 80% optimally (which is very, very respectable in chemistry), what percentage of the potential end yield do you end up with?

Answer: 6.9%.

That's 93.1% of your potential down the pan.

Management is different but I hope you get my point.

Coarsely speaking in my world: RB x RS x RO = RL

(Rubbish Prospecting x Rubbish Selling x Rubbish Operations = Rubbish Life)

Get educated in management.

5. Rubbish Staff
If you have rubbish staff it's your fault. They are the product of your management. The only exception is where you have a bad apple. But if they're still around – it's your fault. Key message - it's your fault and when it isn't, it's still your fault.

6. Not saying "No"
Do not prioritise helping others ahead of turning your own goals into achievements unless these others are paying your bills or dealing with some other fundamental need that keeps you perky and...balanced. Even then...

7. Perfectionism...
...is simply fear of failure, fear of criticism, fear of what you should really be doing and/or self-indulgence dressed up in a fancy suit pretending to be a virtue.

Unmask this imposter before he has his way with you.

8. Being a Monkey Magnet
Perhaps the most nefarious example of 4 and 6 above. Someone else's problem (monkey) is seldom yours. Make sure their monkeys remain firmly on their back.

9. Not eating frogs
Do the worst thing you have to do today first. If you have to eat a frog, eat it. Eat it first.

If you don't, it will gorge on your energy all day, making it bigger, and you still must eat it.

10. Failing to define the next step

If something's on your mind and bothering you it's probably because you have not defined the next thing to do; the next step. So this thing sits there poking you in the ribs every ten minutes until you address it.

So address it.

There's more...being a pessimist...watching TV...I could go on. And on.

Most of us have huge amounts of energy but the energy suckers are legion. Be on guard.

In a Nutshell...
Protect your energy. You're pretty useless without it.

FIVE GREAT WEE QUESTIONS

Apparently January 17th was the most depressing day of the year, according to Dr Arnalls from Cardiff University. He has a formula to work it out based on the weather, debt, money, failed resolutions etc. etc. Hmmm. I assume Cardiff won't be asking for the full £9,000 per annum fees for this sort of tosh.

I'm tempted to bang on about attitude being a choice and the dangers of allowing externalisations like the weather to define your mood, but I won't.

Here's something much better. I often bang on about the need to keep sharpening the saw regularly. This takes some quality time and it should. But in between these sessions, a wee bit of on-the-job sharpening will keep you in top tree-felling form...

So, how to do it?

Ask yourself 5 questions:

1. STOP
What will I stop doing, now?

I have already identified these during my January saw sharpening session. I'm going to add another – stop reading the news so that I don't get riled by stuff like Dr Arnalls' pronouncement. For you, maybe it's a high-payoff activity you hate. Remember, HPAs are critical to goal achievement: they must be done, but not necessarily by you. As long as they're done by someone, all is well.

2. LESS
What shall I do less of?

This is the stuff that does work, but maybe you do too much of it, i.e. you might be being unfocused or disorganised, or some other form of inefficiency. If you raised the quality of something you do, you could get more out of it for less effort. Are you perfectionistic? Remember, the only thing worth being perfectionistic about is your use of time. Nobody cares about the animations on your PowerPoint.

3. MAINTAIN
What shall I keep doing?

This is good stuff that you do well and it works. This is NOT, "oh it's too difficult to change so I'll get to it another day." What's honed, effective, automated, works like a charm...? Great. Be proud.

4. MORE
What shall I do more of?

It's good for me and it works, but I'm a wee bit uncomfortable doing it or it's painful. So I procrastinate, or elevate lesser tasks and get to them first before the important stuff. Madness indeed.

5. START
What shall I start doing?

It's been on my mind for ages but it hasn't bubbled to the surface. Now's the time. Just start. Take the first step. Stop gathering information. Stop waiting for the perfect moment. Start now and monitor results. If you get what you want – great. If not, stop doing it or change what you do. You may even fail to get a result. But that's OK – failing cheaply and quickly is definitely allowed. In fact, it's essential.

Failing slowly and expensively, which you may be doing with the activities you have thought about under items 1 to 4, is NOT allowed. Because that would be depressing.

Thanks to **Peter Thomson (www.PeterThomson.com)** for inspiring this article.

In a Nutshell...

We can keep our saw in tip-top condition by asking ourselves these five wee questions.

How Do Babies Learn To Walk?

I needed a new website, really I did. It had gone beyond nice-to-have and become essential. Not because the existing website is poor, although it is, but because the direction in which I am pushing my business requires a website that plays a much more central role in my lead generation and nurturing efforts.

And I wanted to build it myself. The lead generation role I have in mind for the site requires me to have my hands on the levers and the levers need to be short. I need to be in the car, not driving it by remote-control.

So, despite years of using "refurbishing your website" as an example of what is NOT a high-payoff activity (i.e. critical to goal achievement), I decided the refurbishment of my own website had reached the status of the hallowed high-payoff activity.

And, me being me, I immediately thought of all the things I would need to do to make this website come alive and the fact that I didn't know how to do most of them. All I've ever done before is put these blog posts online and set up a very simple template website.

And, I didn't have a detailed idea of what I wanted.

Hmm. No clear goal and major skill gaps.

There was only one thing to do...
Do something. Anything. Take the first step. Get the car moving. You cannot think a website into existence. Not yet anyway. Once you start you will end up somewhere. If you don't start, you know where you end up.

So I bought a Wordpress theme and I installed it. I had to move the blog. 100+ articles. I hoped there was an easy way to do that. There was. It took 3 minutes. How do you get an image on the sidebar and make it clickable? One minute on Google and it's done.

Installing a video player. Hmmm. Need to deal with the dreaded HTML. Hypertext markup language. It's funny. Computers are great but when you speak to them in their language you realise how fathomless is their stupidity. And let's hope it stays that way.

Anyway the job is done...

...and you are on the new site now.

Here's what I have (re)-learned from this experience –

1. Take the first step.
The end goal does not have to be crystal clear (although it's better if it is) before you take the first step. The entire staircase to the goal does not have to be floodlit before you take the first step. Just like a baby learning to walk - you only need to see the first step.

2. There will be barriers, problems, obstacles.
You have three choices - go round them, through them or allow them to stop you. One of these answers is bad.

3. Things take longer than you think (don't they always).
If you have staff, remember this.

4. Blocktime is essential.
Giving a task large chunks of uninterrupted time is critical. Rome was not built between meetings. I gave myself two solid days to do the videos on the site. It was barely enough. An hour here and an hour there would not have cut it.

5. We get better through repetition.
The videos on this site represent my second foray in this area and I think they are technically much better. Plus, my confidence has soared. This is good (and part of the plan) because there's a lot more videoing coming up very soon and I am sooo glad to have this experience under my belt.

So, there you have it. The infrastructure for the lead generation campaign is in place. It's all mine. I know how all the knobs and levers work and I've added to my skill set and confidence. It took longer than I thought but I don't care.

A website is a small thing at the end of the day. But failing to take the first step is a very big thing. Very big and very bad. Is there a first step you need to take? Define it and put it in your diary. Better yet – do it right now.

In a Nutshell...
Although you may not be able to see every step of your journey, you must take the first step. The route will become clear.

THREE BARRIERS TO TIME MANAGEMENT

I'm always banging on about personal productivity largely because I see so little of it and I know it will make the difference to your work life (and more). Further, most people I meet are not satisfied with their own personal productivity, and those I have helped love it and keep at it.

So, why this huge gap between the massive desire to be more productive (= successful) and the failure to actually achieve it?

Well there's lot of reasons.

For a start we are not taught how to be efficient and effective. At least not in school, when we are at our most habit forming.

Second, a lot of time management material is just garbage. It adopts a year-zero approach — by that I mean the authors pretend that everything that has gone before no longer works because of a) t'internet or b) the recession or c) the author's desire to have you all to themselves.

It's all rubbish of course. And there are many other, external, reasons.

Yes...external reasons. But I think the biggest barriers are in our heads. Internal reasons. And here they are —

"But Mark, time management will kill my spontaneity."
This is a myth. Being productive will not kill your spontaneity or flexibility or creativity. People who are disorganised tend to be busy fools and are not spontaneous. They are often anxious and unfocused. And often chaotic. This is not a good basis for spontaneity or creativity.

The more organised and focused you are, the more relaxed you will be. Then you can be spontaneous.

"But Mark, I'm just a messy person (and I like it)."

This is conditioning. There is no gene for messiness (although I sometimes wonder...). These people have probably been told they are messy, are always late, and never finish what they started. And they grow accustomed to this. They end up liking it. Or they at least arrive at an accommodation with it.

Conditioning works both ways. Personal productivity is learned – like riding a bike. Taking repeated productive action fosters new habits and behaviours. But the system needs to be easy to learn - no 360-page year-zero time management PhD thesis.

"But Mark, I just cannot be productive, I've tried."
This is a self-limiting belief. The thing about beliefs is that people really think of them as truths. They say belief but they mean truth. But it is not a truth. We are not destined to be poor at time management. We are also not destined to be good at it either. Like messiness, there's no time management or personal productivity gene either. It's a learned behaviour. A discipline.

It just depends how much you want it. Which part of the bell-curve you want to be at – really rubbish, rubbish, below average, average, above average, good, great.

It's a choice. In fact, it's a choice we've all already made. But we can re-make the choice. You get another go.

In a Nutshell...
Personal productivity is a choice made by winners.

PLANNING

Fail to plan...
...and you plan to fail. End of story.
You wouldn't pretend to run anything significant without a plan.
Yet some people never plan anything. They waste something much
more important than money. They waste their time. And their time
is the currency they exchange for the chance to realise their
potential...to be what they want to be. A waste indeed.

If you have a job...
...it can be tempting to feel that because you have hired your time
out to your employer, having your time wasted by yourself and
others is not so bad. That only works if you don't want much in
return for hiring out the prime of your life to someone else. Don't
be cheap.

Planning's not for me...
It may not suit you. You may be a smell-the-roses person, in the
moment, not future-focused. Well, the future's focused on you and
it's coming at you, one inexorable second at a time.

Bondage...
You may think plans are constraining. But a plan is not a strait
jacket. Your plan is a roadmap to your desired goal. Your plan may
not withstand first contact with reality, but it's the planning that
counts. When you have a plan, obstacles are smaller, setbacks
more minor. You will find a detour. Your drive and motivation are
higher. You are more win-able; more able to win.

Note to self...
...when was the last time I hit an obstacle in your progress? If you
cannot remember, a siren should be going off in your head. Maybe
you have a do nothing plan. Sometimes this is appropriate. Maybe
in the short-term. Seldom in the medium and beyond-term.

Set goals in stone...

...and plans in the sand. You need to know what your goals are and what you need to do to make them happen – the high payoff activities I go on about incessantly. Then you need to fill your available time with these activities. This is where planning fits...it's the bit between goal setting and achievement. It's about a) defining your high payoff activities and b) making sure you have the space and resources to execute them. That's it. Simple.

Stop the clock...

But you need to be crystal clear on your goals. Don't skip this bit. Without this, you can only plan to get through all the stuff that's already surrounding you. Your to-do list. Then, you are indulging in what is laughably called time management. As if you can manage time.

Take charge...

But if you are clear on your goals, and then plan, plan, plan...then you're not time-managing, you are self-managing.

And in first place we have...

The number one high-payoff activity for everyone is planning. So plan to plan. Schedule time for it. Give it space. You will free up infinitely more time by planning than the planning process itself will consume. Spend time to save time. Planning is the turbo charger on your productivity. Do it yearly, quarterly, monthly, weekly, daily.

So - what to do?

Start small. Plan for tomorrow...today. Ten minutes with your notebook, diary, whatever you use. Write down the high payoff activities that will consume 60 to 70% of your day tomorrow. The things you will do that will deliver what you want, come hell or high water. The things you will do first.

Then, in the morning, pursue these activities with maximum prejudice.

Do you think this will make a difference to you?

In a month?

A year?

A decade?

This is self-management. Maybe it's even self-leadership. Get this right and all is easy.

In a Nutshell...
If you don't have a plan you will be a part of someone else's plan.

My Annual Plan - Best Ever by Miles

I did an interesting exercise the other day. I wrote a list of all my accomplishments. I was thoughtful. I focused on what really matters. I started way back when I was a schoolboy. I wrote them all down. I was surprised by how many there were. It took a wee while.

I don't say this to brag or boast and there are others who I am sure have a much bigger list but that's not the point. My list is my list. I looked at the list and a number of things struck me:

I Did That?

Firstly, I had no idea I'd done all that stuff. I mean of course I know but it isn't front of my mind. What's front of mind is all the blah blah – why did I not win that piece of business? All that stuff. But I look down the list and it makes me feel good. It makes me feel special. And I like feeling special. So I have decided to add my list of accomplishments to my ever expanding positive psychology toolbox.

I am what I do...

Secondly, my accomplishments seem to define me. I am those things. They are the cornerstones of who I think I am. When I think of myself everything I think of is on the list. I am not reliant on being defined by stuff that is, actually, just happenstance, like being Scots, or some nonsense spouted by a boss or a peer or a client.

Loving it...

Thirdly, and most importantly, the list screams passion - I had a passion for everything I achieved. Everything. I really wanted those things. None of it was done as a chore, or under sufferance.

Quick fix...?

Finally, nothing on the list happened overnight. All the achievements took months and some took many years. Years. And there were dark days. Dark months. And this is a key point:

We tend to overestimate what we can do in a year and underestimate what we can do in five years.

That is so important I'm going to say it again –

We tend to overestimate what we can do in a year and underestimate what we can do in five years.

If we are not careful then this can happen - we can get frustrated in the short term and, unless we take the time to survey what we have achieved, then we miss the satisfaction and the motivation that comes from what we have achieved over this longer time horizon. We don't feel as special as often as we should.

Get a plan, man...
So because I want to feel special all the time and have my greatest ever year, I've done this -

Set The Scene
I've listed my accomplishments. The ones that mean something to me. And my strengths and my perceived weaknesses. I remind myself what I am grateful for in my life – yesterday, now and tomorrow. I check myself whenever I have a thought that isn't healthy. You might have some too.

I remind myself that fear is an excuse to do nothing.
I remind myself what I am passionate about because I don't see an accomplishment on my list without passion at the core.

I turn all this into a purpose statement for my life.

Evaluate the Now
I ask myself where I am right now in terms of my satisfaction with five key areas - my mental health; my physical health; my relationships; my finances and my business. Frankly it is not all good. There is stuff that needs changed and has done for some time. I am no paragon of virtue.

Envision the Life of My Dreams
I look again at these five areas and define the perfect outcome for me in each of them. My perfect life. Why not? Why the hell not?

Envision the Year
Then I turn all that jazz into one year goals and associated high-payoff activities and then goals and HPAs for January.

I've written all this down in a workbook. It took me the best part of three days last week (and of course the preceding 47 years of preparation).

Worth its weight in gold...
I feel this workbook is the most valuable thing I own.

It spans forty seven sides of A4.

I feel set up for the forthcoming year like no other year ever and all because I wrote my accomplishments down on a piece of paper and felt inspired...

I wish you an excellent year. Make it your best ever year, as you define it, but do define it. Most people will have just another year or worse – they will allow themselves to be de-railed by the doom-mongers and the naysayers.

But this is not you...
Seize the day. Now is the time.

In a Nutshell...
Taking some significant time out to plan the next year of your life has to be a good idea.

Action

Our brains are brilliant but they are also charged with our protection. We can see wonderful opportunity and possibility, but also the risks and the threats. A large part of our brain simply wants us to stay in our cave. Take no risks. Stay alive.

If you go down to the woods today...
But the risks we face today in 2010 are not as extreme as perhaps they were in 25,000 BC. But our brains apply the same constraint of fear as if we were thinking of taking a walk in the woods, in 25,000 BC, by ourselves, whilst leaving our club behind in the cave, and not noticing the large foot prints in the soil...

We all have...
...a comfort zone. Its limits are defined by our unconquered fears. But here's a thing – your comfort zone cannot stay the same size. It either gets bigger or smaller. It's a clearing in the woods.

I never saw a thing...
Venture into the edge of the woods every day and chop down a few trees. Your clearing is getting bigger. Do nothing and Mother Nature will reclaim what is hers. As you go about your day wandering around your clearing, never getting too close to the edge, you won't see her do her work. But she's doing it, one sapling at a time. Your clearing is getting smaller.

There can be only one...
Fear kills action. Stone dead. Or hobbles it; disables it. But the animosity is mutual. Action kills fear as well. ACTION KILLS FEAR. It's like matter and anti-matter. Fear and action cannot co-exist for long. One or the other will prevail. One will cast the other out into the wilderness.

The fear delusion...

Fear exists. I am fearful of large dogs. I mean really big ones. But fear's PR department has been getting away with murder for centuries...longer. These PR guys have sold us maximum strength, new improved fear when in reality the underlying threats are getting smaller.

It's probably right to be fearful of dinosaurs, less so of making a speech. Boiling lava – yes. Launching a new business – no. Acid-spitting killer ants the size of dinner plates – yes. Picking up the phone – no.

You will not be surprised to know I advocate taking action. Action gets results which lead to new and better actions which lead to new and better results and so it goes on – it's like Darwinism. Evolution for your life. With you in the driving seat. And action is the ignition key...

In a Nutshell...

Fear kills action or action kills fear. Which is it to be with you?

PUBLIC ENEMY NUMBER 1 – LOSS AVERSION

Or...how and why this primal emotion constrains us and what to do about it.

There are few feelings that can actually be measured by psychologists but the feelings we have around loss and gain are two that can be.

Oh My Gawd...
We are twice as upset by loss as we are pleased by gain. I lost a five figure sum (not including the pence) eleven years ago because I didn't do something that would have taken literally 15 seconds.

IT STILL HURTS. ..
This is because of loss aversion – our strong and compelling desire to avoid loss.

This desire is a lizard brain relic – from the time when sabre-toothed tigers roamed the earth and we had more to worry about than slow growth in a top ten economy, I mean, come on.

So this is what normally happens...
We think of something nice we might do.

Say, "I think I'll set up my own business because it will be brilliant." This is a gain. It is good and it feels right. We feel motivated – driven towards all the nice stuff that'll flow from being our own boss and running our own thing.

Then the loss aversion creeps in...
...like a bore at a party. "But I'll lose my regular salary at Scratch & Gouge Ltd" "What about my pension!" "No more Christmas parties." Sorry, that last one's a gain.

That's why when you hear all this guff on the radio – "a poll shows that 75% of nurses/teaches/deep sea divers are thinking of leaving their profession in the next 12 months and taking up competitive macramé", few ever do. The loss aversion freezes them in their tracks (the ones that actually meant it).

We imagine all the losses that walking away from notional security represent and they are very tangible and we feel them twice as much as the less tangible gains of setting up by ourselves so we do....nothing.

We do nothing.

Loss aversion has won...
...we have lost. And there the story ends...

Why do we have such a useless piece of wiring in our heads? Well, who knows? Let's guess - at the end of the day all our psychology is trying to do is to keep us alive long enough to reproduce.

Oh Mother..!
After that, we are pointless in Mother Nature's eyes. So she makes sure we run from the sabre-toothed tiger NOW, even although that cute cave woman over there by the salted mammoth was beginning to look us up and down with that look. That was maybe sensible when we faced death every day. But today the threats we face are seldom life or death and for the latter I think we are now smart enough to spot that level of danger. We don't need the loss aversion automatic protection system. So no thanks Mother Nature. No thanks for loss aversion.

Larkin was right...
...your parents do f*** you up.

But...
...the 21st Century human can overcome this poor wiring. We cannot upgrade our brains (sadly). But we can apply a patch. A fix.

The story isn't over...
Here's what to do - reclassify the risks in, for example, chucking in our job and setting up our company, as "small and survivable". Because they are. Compared to a risk with a high likelihood of death or irretrievable financial damage, what we're talking about here is small and survivable. We will not die. It's just that our brain is telling us that's what we're up against because our brain is very good at catastrophising. It's designed that way.

Health Warning here people...
...we need to use our judgement in risk assessment. Chucking in your job has small and survivable risks. Going over the Niagara Falls in a barrel has large and potentially non-survivable risks. If you have a nagging feeling that you have the judgement of a C-list celeb on coke, seek advice from your more sensible friends.

Assuming...
...our risks do in fact have small and survivable risks, then we can see them in context and refocus on the huge positive motivation that naturally flows from the potential we can see in our first thought – setting up our own business or whatever it may be.

Understand loss aversion for what it is (a relic), and your motivation can act unencumbered and then you have truly defeated one of life's greatest foes. Well done you.

In a Nutshell...
Fear of loss is extremely powerful and leads to inaction. But the risk of loss is usually small and survivable.

What's In It For Me?

You should ask yourself this question often, especially when I decide to do nothing...

"What's in it for me?"
It seems very direct, very...un-British.

Well, what's in it for me?
The raise, the promotion, the bonus, the whatever-it-is.

It's good to know what you will get for what you do.

It's positive...

We tend to think of what we get as the reward for an action. And we usually direct the question to others, because they are doing the giving...

But let's turn it around...
Here's one from my early days in self-employment...

I need to make twenty cold calls per day.

Yikes...
What's in it for me?

"Well, I will find clients and that will be good because then I'll be able to pay my bills."

Hmmmm...OK. The snowy peaks of Maslow's Pyramid are hardly being penetrated with that are they?

I hated making those calls and sometimes I didn't make them because I didn't want to. Then the next day I'd ask myself again – What's in it for me?

"Well, I will find clients and that's good and it will get my business going and"…yeah, yeah, yeah.

Some days I got it really right (although it took about three years) – I'll get lots of clients, then money, giving less stress, less pressure, more freedom, a self-sustaining business making money without me turning up, financial freedom….weeeee-heeeee….you know the trajectory.

Great and positive stuff indeed.

So far so obvious…
OK. Here's the bit I've been missing…

I NEVER ASKED MYSELF WHAT WAS IN IT FOR ME WHEN I CHOSE TO SUBMIT TO MY FEARS AND NOT DO WHAT I KNEW I HAD TO.

I think I'll say that again because it looks good here on my screen - I NEVER ASKED MYSELF WHAT WAS IN IT FOR ME WHEN I CHOSE TO SUBMIT TO MY FEARS AND NOT DO WHAT I KNEW I HAD TO.

We never judge the status quo…

But we should, because there *is* something in the status quo for you. It's just that it's usually a bit rubbish. If we liked the status quo we'd still be living in caves.

Let's try it…
"I am not going to make those calls because I don't want to. I am not comfortable doing it and I hate it. This task is like a millstone around my neck…"

"What's in *that* for me?"

Well what's in that for me is the destiny of those other wild-eyed dreamers who pursue the siren call of self-employment - 70 hours weeks and a mediocre salary. Spending more and more time doing the same stuff in the vain belief that doing more of what doesn't work will miraculously turn out to be the stuff that does work! No, no, no, no, no.....

I love Mondays...

OK it's another Monday. I don't know about you but it felt like yesterday when I sat down and planned this year. Now it's October 10th. Wot?

I've been using the "what's in it for me?" technique when faced with the less glam tasks for five weeks now and it really works.

It's allied to the question I ask my coaching clients in goal setting – "what bad stuff will be avoided if you achieve your goal?" But it's a wee bit punchier than that.

We conceptualise the good stuff that flows from positive action pretty easily. But we struggle to crystallise the bad stuff that will come from our inaction.

So - what to do?

There are consequences to everything we do, including deciding to not do something.

Starting now...when you find yourself taking avoiding action on something you know you should do but don't want to and you're getting comfortable with that decision...ask yourself...

"This decision to do nothing - *what's in it for me?*"

In a Nutshell...

We never ask what the consequences are of inaction. They are usually very unexciting, at best.

PROCESS

You don't stand a snowball's chance in hell of achieving anything in any organisation unless you have systematised everything you can.

When I was a young boy...
...I travelled across the Pennines to work in north Manchester at ICI, Purchasing and Supply. My first commercial job. This department was ISO registered. There was a procedure for everything. I didn't know the first thing about purchasing and I wasn't going to ask anyone. Oh no! Not me.

I worked every day and then, in the evening, when everyone had gone home, I read the procedures – 2 hrs a night. After two months, I knew how purchasing and supply worked. It did nothing for my negotiating skills, or commercial brain. But that's not what procedures are for.

It takes two...
The skills part lies parallel to the procedure. One is not a substitute for the other.

Without skills, flexibility, experience and creativity: the procedure is a hollow shell.

Without procedure: skills and experience remain largely untapped.

My background has...
...largely been in manufacturing. It's highly regulated. We had procedures for most things – manufacturing, health and safety, HR, how to walk to your office with a hot drink...

...except sales and marketing.
Except sales and marketing. Oh yes. Sales people are creative, dynamic. They have the gift of the gab, they are flight of foot. They are supreme; saviours of the business. You cannot tether this sort of mercurial talent with procedures. Procedures are for the little people. The office-bound dullards, with their chit-chat about last night's telly.

This is, of course, rubbish.

I have a dirty secret...

It's staggering that so many sales and marketing people have managed to largely get away with not being proceduralised; not using a systematic process. I was one of them. Here's a dirty secret – sales and marketing is a process. Sales people and marketing people are not born. You don't need special talents. You don't need the gift of the gab unless you're selling from a market stall. You're not doing that, are you?

Today's winners...

...don't allow the critical functions of sales and marketing to be anarchic. They understand it is one of the business' core processes; the key word being process.

In marketing...

...they understand their Target Market Segments, their Ideal Customer Profile, and how to get to them. They understand their Value Proposition and their Unique Selling Proposition. And they act accordingly. They don't spend a penny piece on any form of marketing communications unless the return-on-investment can be rapidly calculated. They do marketing experiments – cheap and quick. If it works; do more. If it doesn't; stop. It's a process.

If you run your own business and you do not have systematised marketing (i.e. getting those who are interested in what you do to come to you without you hunting them down, one-by-one; your life will be a misery.)

In sales...

...they know how to prospect (and why); how to sell; how to close; how to deliver; how to resell; how to ask for referrals. And when and why all these things should be done. It is not left to chance. They do them all, all the time. It's not left to what the sales rep feels like doing today. It's a process.

Of course skill and flair and all that other stuff are important; and with all else being equal they will win the day. But I'd rather have six solid guys following a process, than six prima-donnas who don't know what day of the week it is, but they're great guys you know...customers love 'em.

Too many people...

...spend most of their time unfocussed, unguided, goalless, on autopilot, distracted, anxious, fearful and doing the wrong things for the wrong reasons at the wrong times. OK I exaggerate a wee bit, but not so much.

They certainly spend most of their time doing the one thing they think is important that they are comfortable doing. This is not enough.

I have seen the light...

People can achieve great things. They have the potential. Challenge your colleagues, bosses and subordinates to develop processes for what they do. Because it's the foundation that allows their brilliance to shine every day, not just on the occasional day when the chaos allows it.

In a Nutshell...

In business, almost everything is a process and if it isn't it isn't reliable and if it isn't reliable you should replace it with a process.

PROCESS – PART II

Lights out...

I bought my current home about ten years ago. I had the house completely redecorated from top to bottom. Now, in the bathroom, there are 6 halogen spotlights in the ceiling. Every twelve months or so, when one bulb pops, the others also pop within about two days. This has been going on for a decade. It's the same in the kitchen.

I drove three examples of the same model of car. The water pump failed on each at the same mileage, plus or minus 3%.

I have two televisions in my house. One is 29 years old and the other 22 years old. Both work fine (although they are somewhat bulky).

Before 1980, air passenger fatalities varied between 1 and 2 per billion passenger kilometres flown. Since 1980, it's been zero, give or take.

It never used to be like this. I remember lying in bed as a schoolboy listening to my Dad trying to start the car. The new car. Thank you British Leyland. I remember when light bulbs used to fail at random, and often. Things would break. Clocks would stop. Planes would fall out of the sky.

What's going on..?

What's happened in manufacturing over the last few decades is amazing. The processes companies use to make stuff have been analysed, defined and managed to ensure that every item that is made, as far as is practical and merited by its importance, is the same as the one before, and the one after. That's why the lights and the water pump fail at the same time (after a long time) and my TVs haven't failed at all. And mechanical failure in planes is so infrequent.

Genius..!

No more Quality Control (sifting out the inferior stuff and throwing it away, along with what it cost to make). Now we have Quality

Assurance (making sure we understand our processes so that we don't make rubbish in the first place.) Genius!

Not just for stuff...

But it's so much wider. It's not just about product quality. Almost everything is a process. You need a process to understand where you're going (strategy). You need a process to make it happen (operational strategy, usually marketing and one other key process, perhaps project management, or whatever it is that delivers your value). You need a process to get the very best from your most able people (personal productivity).

That is not to preclude creativity (here's a newsflash – creativity is a process as well. The reason most people prevent themselves from being creative is because they fear looking foolish.)

Not convinced..?

You may think this is tosh. You may think there's some special foo-foo dust that delivers your results. That's not management. That's hope. And as they say, hope is not a method. Hope is not a process.

As W Edwards Deming said, "If you can't describe what you are doing as a process, you don't know what you're doing."

What's for lunch...

Without defining the critical processes that will turn your dreams into reality, you're at monumental risk from any competitor who does define these processes. They will eat your lunch and anything else they fancy.

Having great people is necessary but not sufficient. Do you have well-meaning people who never quite hit the heights? Their attitude is good, they have sufficient IQ points, they do the hours, but they never set the heather alight. They never sparkle.

What's wrong with them? Well, it's probably their manager. The manager who doesn't see the road to success as being the excellent execution of a few well-honed processes. The manager who believes in foo-foo dust.

In a Nutshell...
Success is a process.

How To Stop Making It Up As You Go Along

It was 1991...
I drove across the M62 for a job interview. If I got the job it would be my pass out of the lab and into the glittering commercial world. A senior buyer. For ICI Pharmaceuticals, now AstraZeneca. I had a PhD in chemistry and 3 years lab experience. I was a shoo-in for a commercial job, surely. What could go wrong?

All I had to do was find the exit for the M66, do a few simple left/right manoeuvres, and I'd be there. I found the exit. I got on the M66. It took me north. This was not right. I needed to go south. No problem. Off at the next exit, straight back on and boom, everything would be OK. So I got off at the next exit but it wasn't a full junction...it just took me around onto some dual carriageway and I was lost in space.

I got to the interview...
...45 Minutes late. I was shaken, but not stirred.

I got the job.

OK here's the point...
The buying department I joined was ISO registered.

That means that everything they did was systematised – proceduralised. It was all written down. The documents were called SOPs – standard operating procedures.

All the procedures were lined up in files on a book case. I'd say about 30 feet of files. A lot of SOPs. But it was all there. A mere handful of people buying everything needed for a manufacturing business turning over more than a billion quid in sales in the 1990s and everything they did was all written down.

And I read them...
It took me about two months. But at the end of it I was a buyer. Green? Yes. Able to do the job? Yes!

I am reminded of this because I have been meaning to get around to mastering LinkedIn as a source of prospects and customers. But I was being tactical. I was doing this, and then that. No process. No procedure. No consistency. No measures of performance. Basically, I was playing at it. Messing around.

I needed an SOP...
So I did my research on current best practice – even spent some money to shorten my learning curve (because keeping your money and spending your time to re-invent a wheel is dumb, dumb, dumb).

I reduced it all down to the essence. Like making a good chicken stock.

First – there's one-off set up activities. Then daily, weekly, monthly and quarterly tasks. Consistently applied with measures.

I have called my SOP LinkedIn SOP v 1.0. Catchy – eh? It's a single side of A4. Total effort involved to execute the procedure is 15 minutes per day. I have already seen an improvement. Got more new members to my Business Owners Group (yes – B.O.G., I know) in the last week than in the last month.

It's a simple example...
...but I suggest that if we find ourselves doing important yet repetitive tasks at a mostly tactical level without a plan in the background, then it might be a good idea to take a step back, get strategic, then tactical, and then implement and, after a while, look at your measures and adjust the tactics accordingly until you get what you want.

This is how to deal with high-payoff activities: finding prospects, getting referrals, preparing for major presentations, pitching for follow-on work...whatever you do. Reduce it to an SOP. Measure your performance and make changes.

And...consider if you can delegate or outsource the actual work. Anything you see from me with my name at the bottom will always be written by me but there are elements to my LinkedIn SOP that are simply a chore and I don't need to do them. They just need to be done. And there are multitudes on www.elance.com who can do those parts for me. And then I'll have more time to write stuff like this.

In a Nutshell...

Most work is a process. If you define it as such you will do better work and have some time left over to be more strategic.

PART 2
WHAT YOU NEED TO KNOW –
STRATEGY, MANAGEMENT,
LEADERSHIP AND PEOPLE

Emotional Intelligence

Leadership

Trust

Culture

Beware of Groupthink!

How to Persuade People to Do What You Want

Teams

Thinking

Zero Tolerance of Poor Performance

How to Listen

What to Do In Meetings

How to Have a Senior Team Meeting

The Key to Negotiation

Part 1 got us up and running, applying the knowledge we have productively to the achievement of our goals. Now we have some time to add to and refine our knowledge. In this part, I have included what I think are the fundamentals for success in any organisation. They are the basics of strategy, management and leadership and what it takes to be professional with other people, whether they work for you or not.

9 Hard Questions For Your Business

Here goes...

Jim Collins says, in **Good to Great: Why Some Companies Make the Leap - And Others Don't,** that you must ask some tough questions about your business if you are going to achieve your goals.

So here are 9 tough questions (some are groups of questions) I'm going to ask myself right now...

1. How do I make money (cashflow)? What do I sell and to whom? Why do they buy? How do I gain new customers? Those that don't buy – why not? What do I sell that isn't worth the effort? What's my gross margin, operating margin, profitability and cashflow on everything I do? This is about gaining absolute clarity on my current position – no fuzzyness, no supposition.

2. Which relationships in business, both inside and outside my company, are critical to my success. Am I nurturing them accordingly?

3. Which relationships in business, both inside and outside my company, are holding me back sufficiently that I should terminate them?

4. Does my company routinely generate positive cashflow? There was a guy on Radio 4 the other day bemoaning the fact that he could no longer meet payroll because the overdraft he routinely used to fill his cashflow "gaps" had been withdrawn by his bank. He felt hard done to. Wrong. You're bust pal. No cash flow = dead. It was only a matter of time.

5. What are my major avenues for gaining new customers? Are they fully costed? Remember, my time is my greatest asset. I meet lots of people who don't value their time. That's not true. They do value their time...they actually value it at zero. Time certainly has no cost (there is lost opportunity cost of course). But it does have a value. You should

value your time at no less than £400/day (£100K pa) as an absolute minimum and probably much more. You might not earn that yet but you're worth it, right?

6. What's the average lifetime value of my customers? This tells me how much I can spend to find a new customer. How can I market without knowing this?

7. What's the acquisition cost of a new customer? Once I have this answer, combined with the previous answer, the size of my opportunity is defined by the number of potential customers I have and my ability to generate cash from one existing customer to turn the next potential customer into a real one...and so it goes on.

8. If I was filmed 24/7 for a week by a BBC film crew what would I do more of, and less of, than normal. Self-management is critical. Am I taking positive steps to improve myself – read more, learn more, do more, take time to think, reflect and make changes? Am I productive, not just busy? Am I purposeful, focused and thoughtful at all times? Am I getting better (almost) every day? Do I invest in myself?

And, finally, the toughest question...

9. Do I find these questions positively challenging and exciting...or frightening and best avoided?

In a Nutshell...
In any business there are 9 tough questions to ask. If there is no answer or a poor answer to any of them, this constitutes a significant business risk that could break you.

STRATEGY

Hello Big Boy...
Strategy is not just for the big guys. Small businesses need one as well. And it doesn't have to be a 200 page tome. And it doesn't need consultants.

What is a strategy...?
It's your purpose. Your direction. It contains your vision and mission. It states your competitive advantage (or makes you get one if you don't have one). The markets you are in. And more.

This applies to you.

And your team...
Strategy binds people with good attitude together under a common purpose. A higher level, compelling, challenging, achievable purpose.

Links in a chain...
The output of strategy is strategic objectives. This could be..... "put a man on the moon before this decade is out". Or it could be "find 5 new profitable customers in the hotel sector by year end".

And these objectives are linked to the plans that deliver the strategic objectives...marketing objectives, operational objectives, technology objectives...

You may need to pull all these together to put a man on the moon. If your goals are more modest, you may just need to find an effective marketing channel. Or hire a telemarketer.

And the chain continues...
...into individual objectives for leaders, managers and staff. Or just you if you are all three.

The point is you are now in goal-directed action mode. You have a target, a destination, and you can walk or run, depending on your level of ambition.

It doesn't matter who you are – you're either on the right road or you're not. Marshalling thousands of people and billions of quid, or just your own time...

That's why you need a strategy.

So how to do it...?

Start with the end in mind. What's the output of a strategy? I'd say approximately four objectives max, for the next year... four things that, if you achieve them will have taken you forward (assuming you want to go forward of course). Objectives that, once achieved, will make you feel proud, make you happy. Make you feel in control, purposeful and productive.

Tool up...

There are some tools that are as old as the hills.

A **SWOT analysis** to measure your strengths, weaknesses, opportunities and threats. Strengths and opportunities combine to tell you where the money is, right now. Act on this first. Weaknesses and threats need to be plugged, but later.

A *competitive force analysis* – which tells you which of the four business strategies you really should have (some say this is simplistic, or old-fashioned, but it holds true for the majority of businesses and if you're not clear on which one of these strategies you have, you are going to get eaten alive from both ends at the same time).

The *Ansoff matrix* puts real context into your product/market mix and the associated risks.

Get my free list of 372 strategy tools...
No. There are many others, but there are only about ten that have widespread relevance and I suspect about four that really apply to you. Less is more.

These tools are simple, easy to understand and can be done on the back of a fag packet.

Once you've done this (spend no more than one hour), you should be able to construct 3 to 5 strategic objectives for your business.

Then you have purpose. And your actions can be goal-directed. And whether you choose to walk or run, at least you're on the right road.

In a Nutshell...
Strategy is purpose. This is not a luxury.

WHAT STEVE JOBS TAUGHT ME

I've just finished reading Walter Isaacson's biography of Steve Jobs (Santa – take note – *I have read it*). It's an authorised biography but neither Jobs nor anyone else had any editorial control, or even any foresight.

Jobs predicted he'd read it a few years after it came out. That's not going to happen.

Let's get something out of the way here – this is no hagiography. Jobs, as a person, comes out of it looking pretty bad. It's warts-and-all and the warts are many.

He had no filter between his brain and his mouth and he knew it and he didn't care.

But – he did amazing things and there will be few of us who do not own at least one of his products or have seen one of his movies. (I've seen them all.)

So, what can we learn from this book that we can apply to our businesses?

Be Lacking in Screws
This is all about product excellence. I think it applies to service as well.

Jobs was driven to make the best consumer products it was possible to make. That's it. That's the mission statement. He saw the early hobbyist computers as clunky, unintegrated (some didn't even come with a box around them – they were bare exposed circuit boards, and no power supply!). Essentially unusable to anyone bar the expert hobbyist.

Later he saw PCs as bland, shoddy, cobbled together contraptions containing barely compatible components and clunky software. The user experience was poor.

It was the same with portable music players and phones...techie products made for techies where their lack of usability was almost a point of pride to their engineers.

Jobs went to unbelievable lengths to make his products feature rich, very beautiful and incredibly simple to use. And he managed it. He gave complete solutions. With no screws. You cannot get inside an Apple product and you don't need to.

I believe Jobs was truly not interested in money. He believed that to focus on making money was the end for an organisation. It was better to focus on delivering value excellently, i.e. in Apple's case, through truly excellent products. And this makes sense to me because making stuff is an input that we can control. Making money is an output that is only indirectly controlled.

He did no market research because he wasn't into incremental product development. He was into blowing the competition out of the water. He quotes Henry Ford – "if I'd asked my customers what they wanted they'd have said 'a faster horse'."

This allowed him to demand premium prices. Despite having only 7% of the computer market by unit sales, Apple in 2010 was pulling in 35% of the entire segment's operating profit.

Be Intense
This is about focusing on as few projects as possible.

It was usual for the entire organisation, one of the biggest companies on earth, to be working on no more than three products at any one time.

If you are going to make the very best products you can, you can't be developing fifty of them. Know your limits.

Be More Than Just A Protest Singer
This is about innovation.

Jobs loved Bob Dylan and he said that Dylan couldn't sing protest songs all his life – he had to move on and he did. Innovation ran through everything Jobs did – from the *Gorilla Glass* screen on the iPhone to the design of the Apple Stores. From business model innovation (iTunes Store) to reinventing animated movies.

And even then, innovation sometimes only gets you so far, as the plethora of smart phones out now will show.

But not innovating is not an option.

Be As One
This is about organisational structure.

Jobs felt Apple could get stuff done like no other company because there was no silo mentality in the organisation. He looked at Sony who had made the WalkMan and they had all the skills to make the iPod/iTunes/iTunesStore integrated product suite that has reshaped (and saved) the music industry, but they couldn't get it together because the music and technology *divisions* had conflicting priorities and would not talk to each other.

Let's remember what the word *division* actually means – *the state of being divided.*

Apple has only one P&L which is amazing for an organisation of its size. And everyone involved in product development feels an allegiance to the product, not a division.

There's more, much more, but these are four of the major pillars upon which Apple was built. There are lessons here for a lot of us.

In a Nutshell...
Great vision and massive action is a heady brew...

How To Be like Richard Branson

I was watching something the other day about Richard Branson and his private retreat in the Caribbean - Necker Island. Apparently he really does live in this paradise. It's thousands of miles from anywhere so I guess Richard's work doesn't require him to turn up to get paid.

It made me think of my own journey – what I've done and what I've yet to do. I managed to boil it down into four stages. Your stages may be different, or maybe you have yet to consider your potential stages, but I think the general "flow" is common.

Stage 1 – Employment.
Yes. Done this and got the tee-shirt and then left it in a hotel somewhere along with my Blackberry charger. But no worries. I put the loss on expenses.

Employment taught me a lot. And paid me a lot...relatively. But in return I gave my employers my life, which they did not ask for but I gave it to them anyway. Staying in the game took a lot out of me. This is common.

And I stayed an employee for too long. But four years ago I finally made it over the barbed wire fence and into...

Stage 2 – Self-Employment.
This is where I am now. It's just like employment only with the added spice of terror, at least at the start. The terror lasted for about two years which seems to be remarkably typical for those who escape.

But now I've got self-employment "sorted" and I simply feel a low-level paranoia that is rapidly becoming my best friend. But a friend I do not need...

So what is self-employment? I employ myself. I have a job. Like before. I know what my value to others is – it isn't some dumb discussion framed by a corporate remuneration policy. It is precisely what people pay me. No more. No less. There's nowhere to hide. It is stark.

I am enjoying it. But I am enjoying it in the way I enjoy a 35 mile cycle. It's good when you stop. So I need to stop self-employment.

Which is funny, because self-employment feels very grown up. But it isn't really. Because there's more. Much more...

Stage 3 – Running Your Business.
There are two key words here that require definition. Business = an organisation that makes the owner money. Running = you manage those who create the value on a day-to-day basis. You do not get involved in any heavy lifting, or operational delivery.

On a day-to-day basis the business makes money with or without you.

Once at Stage 3, you may decide to turn up every day – that's OK but that is not the point. The point is there is an organisation that makes money without you doing any operational tasks.

If you went away for 8 weeks your sales wouldn't fall.

I am at the Stage of leaping from Stage 2 to Stage 3.

Next we have...

Stage 4 – Not Running Your Business.
This is where Richard Branson is. It is true enlightenment. It is freedom. True freedom. Not the "£300K salary, £1m bonus, house in Chelsea, Heathrow on a Sunday morning, I earn a fortune yet I still manage to spend it." That's not freedom. That's gilded cage.

No.

Freedom is "not having to be somewhere, being barefoot on the beach, clear headed, surrounded by those you love, centred and calm, beholden to no one, utterly in control."

The money comes in courtesy of the great people and the superb systems you have put in place.

If you went away for 8 months, revenue would not fall. At least not solely because you were absent.

You have separated what you do with your time from what you do for your money. Now this kind of freedom may seem unattainable but it isn't.

This is not about a money-fixation. It's not about having gazillions of cash in the bank. It's not about Ferraris and executive jets. Although it could be, if that floats your boat. But it doesn't have to be about that. It's about making money *not* the issue, rather than *the* issue.

You just need to do this –
Set up a few automatic (OK – semi-automatic) money streams that, in total, cover your current costs of living on this earth.

There are a huge number of ways this can be done, if you actually have some bloody value to offer.

Then the game reduces to turning your genuine value into money...and that's marketing.

That's it.

It's called financial freedom.

Cast aside your chains.

You will need to make some interventions in your operation from time to time of course, but you don't need to dig holes every day to get paid.

And the scale doesn't have to be massive - you don't need an airline or a mobile network unless you have some serious habits. And I've just been on **www.caribbeanislandbrokers.com** and you'd be surprised at how cheap your own little atoll could be. (Note to self – "am I allowed to establish my own country?")

I'm not at Stage 4 yet. That's three years away.

But it's on my radar and right now, I need to make the jump to Stage 3.

Can't wait.

I can feel the sand under my feet...and the joy of not having to turn up to be paid, so that I can get on with my proper life's work and show my kids that there is another way...

What fun.

In a Nutshell...
There are four stages of evolution. Only the last one delivers true freedom.

BE YOUR OWN MANAGEMENT CONSULTANT

They say the smart guys know all the answers. This is true. But the really smart guys know all the questions.

You don't need any management consultants to help you in your company. Be your own trusted advisor. Ask yourself these simple questions –

1. What can we do?

This is about core competencies. What can your organisation do in its sleep? What's it been doing for years? What do you excel at? Be honest. Richard Branson's core competence is the assessment, selection and execution of business ideas. Nothing to do with planes. Or music.

2. What's happening in our market?

Is it expanding or contracting? Is it profitable? Is it cyclical? Where are prices going? Costs?

But you must segment your market. A segment is a part of the market that buys in the same way. Think airport parking – there's executive parking at £30/day, all the way through to offsite parking at £20 a week for the happy holidaymaker. I reckon at Manchester airport there's at least 5 segments of airport parking. Each segment will pay different amounts for different services. And broadly, the mass market segment (mass = many people) generates low margin per person, but there's lots of them. The niche market (£30/day execs) generates high profits per person, but there's fewer of them. And the costs to service them are different.

So, what is happening in your market? – by segment.

3. What does our competition look like?

Again, segment-wise. What's your USP, by segment. Focus on underserved segments. Who isn't getting what they need? Ryanair saw a mass market for low cost airfares all around Europe. In fact what they probably saw was Southwest Airlines doing it in the States. So they copied them. Fair enough.

4. What are the economics of our market from our customer's viewpoint?

Well before Ryanair you got all sorts of stuff bundled in that you wouldn't have paid for if they'd been offered to you separately – bad coffee, bad wine, bad sandwich. Now, you can pretty much avoid all additional costs if you want to (although being charged for unavoidable services, like check-in, simply annoys).

5. What are the economics from our perspective?

For Ryanair it's maximising the asset utilisation of the fleet (i.e. keeping the planes in the air as close to 24/7 as possible) and driving costs down (which is why "Glasgow Airport" is in fact at Prestwick Airport, because the latter's landing charges are lower.) Also, what are the effects of scale across your value chain? For that matter, what is your value chain?

Keep asking yourself these questions until you convince yourself you know the real, insightful answers. It is often just one new insight that changes the game, and not just in big companies. I had a client who was selling a software product face-to-face. The product price was £50. This doesn't work. A new distribution model was needed. Now it works. Simple? Yes – when you see it.

Nobody built PCs to order before Dell. But think of the advantages – customers feel they get an exclusive service (to an extent). They get to buy exactly what they want (and probably end up buying more than they need). Dell do not put the value-adding bit in (assembly) until the cash from the customer is in the bank and they never end up with the perennial problem faced by technology hardware businesses - masses of obsolete stock.

Go on. Spend a day as your own management consultant. Could be the most profitable day you ever have.

In a Nutshell...
Having good answers to these strategic questions sets you up for success.

GROWTH

Igor Ansoff was a Russian-American who is lauded as the father of Strategic Management.

His most famous contribution is his eponymous matrix, which helps firms decide what their product and market growth strategy will be.

It comes to my mind because I've spoken to a number of leaders recently who want to do very different things to what they are doing now. This may be right for them. But the grass is always greener on the other side of the fence. And the fence is often topped with razor wire. And the field beyond is a minefield.

The Ansoff Matrix looks at products and markets – both existing and potential new ones.

Stick to the knitting...Market Penetration
Growing by selling your existing products into your existing markets is called market penetration.

Market penetration can seem boring – the same old stuff. But wait – you know what you're doing. You already make these products (or services). You already understand the markets. You're already there. You can do more of what you're already doing. You know you can. You can make things more difficult for your competitors. You can sell more, more often, to more people, for more money. Importantly, it's low risk.

Some managers want to move away from market penetration because there are environmental issues looming that will make their existing market much tougher. But remember – markets don't disappear, competitors do. Someone will win – you can make sure it's you, in this lowest risk growth area.

Examples of market penetration? They are legion. Nokia, Ericsson etc. – all the telecoms companies.

Risk rating – low. No bullets to dodge here.

Now with wings...Product Development
Growing by selling new products into your existing markets is called product development.

You've got some fabby new products and you want to sell them to your existing markets. The key issue here is how expensive is it to develop new products. If you can knock these out inexpensively, this is a great strategy and is not much riskier than market penetration. If your new products take time to develop, and money, and then fulfil some critical role in your customers business, like maybe a new aero engine, then there's a real risk.

Example – most healthy companies most of the time. Supermarkets selling, eh, everything...insurance, banking. What does it look like when it goes wrong? – car company recalls.

Risk rating – low to medium. Death unlikely, but possible.

Just arrived from the UK...Market Development
Growing by selling your existing products into markets that are new for you is called market development.

OK, so you decide to sell your widgets into a new market. Lots and lots of lovely new customers. What could be better? The new market is huge. If we get 2% we'll be rich. Yes, but that 2% already belongs to someone. And they want to keep it. You'll have to fight. And they know the territory.

This is a higher risk strategy. It might be the right thing to do. But you better make sure you've done your market research, and you have a USP that's watertight, airtight and extremely shiny.

Example – Lucozade – I remember my Gran drinking it when she was ill. Now it's a sports drink!

Risk rating – low to medium. Death unlikely, but more likely that with market development.

All change...Diversification
And finally, growing by selling new products into markets that are new to you is called diversification.

I've got a great idea. I've spotted this great new market that's growing like topsy. We can make loads of new products, go over there, sell them and make a killing! We'll all be rich. What could possibly go wrong? How difficult can it be to understand this new market? We're smart guys.

This strategy has all the other risk factors combined, and some. To make it work you need to get an awful lot of stuff right. In order to speed the process of getting into new markets with new products, companies often go on an acquisition spree...

Example – GEC/Marconi. Was in defence, diversified into telecoms. Total car crash. Value of £34 billion reduced to £66 million. Board members last seen skulking around the US, hoping nobody Googles their names).

Risk factor – running with scissors, with your shoe laces tied together. In the dark.

No risk, no reward...
It's all about managing the risk in your growth strategy. Risks are not to be avoided. They are to be understood and managed.

But remember, the greatest risk is having no growth strategy.

Example – a lot of wee companies.

Risk rating – Russian Roulette.

In a Nutshell...
Growth is great but has risks which you must manage.

Is It Time To Fire Yourself Out of a Cannon?

There's two guys. Each is standing on a box and holding one end of the same rope. The rope is ten feet off the ground. Your mission, should you choose to accept it, is to get over the rope.

How do you do it? (You cannot tickle them to get them to lower the rope.)

Well, you could get a big step ladder, climb up and jump over. Or you could use a trampoline. Or, if you have the technique, you could pole vault. Or Fosbury Flop yourself over the rope.

Each of these approaches has their pros and cons. They will have their own relative success rates. Some need equipment – a trampoline, a pole. Some do not. But the point is they all work.

So far so good.

Now, the rope is one hundred feet in the air. Don't ask me how the guys did this, but they did.

How do you get over it? Trampoline? Step ladder? No. You need a new approach. Maybe a helicopter; or you could build a staircase; or fire yourself out of a cannon; or use a jet pack.

The point is the approaches that get you over the ten foot high rope don't work with the one hundred foot high rope. They may work with a fifteen foot high rope, or maybe even a twenty foot high rope, but there will come a time when they are not up to the job. The current processes, technologies and approaches only get you so far. To hit the heights – the one hundred foot high rope - you need new means.

It's the same in business. Whatever it is you do now...your marketing; your strategising; your productivity; your product and service development; how you deliver your value; your logistics; your systems and processes; everything that makes up your business, or department: each is either -

a) Inadequate

It can hardly get you over a one foot rope, never mind a ten foot rope. Your trampoline has lost its spring. Your Fosbury is more of a Fop than a Flop. Or,

b) Adequate

Adequate for your needs. Not over-engineered, or creaking at the seams. Sufficient. It does the job. It is reliable. Fit for purpose. Or,

c) Over-engineered.

It can get you over the one hundred foot rope. Even although you can see only the ten foot rope. This may be a good thing as you are prepared for the future. Or it may just be a cost, because helicopters are more expensive than trampolines.

You will probably have a mix of a, b and c in your business/organisation.

Here are some critical questions –

Q1 What do you do today to generate sales?

Q2 Can these activities generate a five-fold increase in sales?

Q3 If not, what changes do you have to make to these activities, or what new activities do you have to adopt to generate a five-fold increase in sales?

Q4 If you imagine increasing your sales five-fold over the next 2 to 5 years, what supporting systems and processes in your business will become inadequate and in what order?

Q5 How will you deal with the answer to Q4?

If you take the time to answer these five questions thoughtfully you will end up with the bones of a good growth strategy. You will be getting ready for the one hundred foot rope.

In a Nutshell...
There comes a point when doing more of the same no longer propels you forward. Then, you will need to do different things.

MANAGEMENT

It is worth remembering that a lot of what we take for granted and value (law, democracy, capitalism) are not naturally occurring, like sunshine and rain, but have in fact been arrived at by debate and thought over the centuries and millennia. Going back to these first principles can often be interesting.

Management is no different...
Henri Fayol is generally considered the father of what was called planning. Today, I think it would be called management.

Fayol offered some key principles for transforming businesses. This is essentially his management philosophy:

1. Division of work – this is about allowing people to specialise, to do what they are good at with minimal associated garbage like box ticking.

2. Authority – management's right to manage. This country is a democracy, but the workplace isn't. If you are respected and respectable, you may get a tacit vote, but this is not a right.

3. Discipline – employees must obey (but will not do so in the face of poor leadership). Leaders need to remember you can condition people very quickly – if you allow indiscipline to go unremarked, you will quickly find more of it that you can handle, and it will be your fault. I don't operate a no-blame culture in these pearls – it will be your fault.

4. Unity of command – one boss only please. With two bosses, someone always gets abused. Sometimes the subordinate, but in my experience usually one or both of the managers.

5. Subordination of individual interest – the goals of the firm are always paramount. If you have some prima ballerinas, and you are not

running a dance troupe, you have a problem. They're going for self-actualisation and sending you the bill.

6. Remuneration – payment is an important motivator (I know they love working here but they wouldn't turn up if you didn't pay them. And neither would you.)

7. Line of authority – you need a hierarchy. Worker's co-ops have failed to take over the world for a reason.

8. Equity – kindliness and justice is required. Absolutely, and the effective worker being treated the same as the ineffective worker looks like an injustice to both. But only one of them is laughing.

9. Stability of tenure - always good but no fur-lined ruts please. Dead wood is the fastest growing tree I've ever seen.

10. Initiative – allow it, but you need a process (see 5 above). This is a workplace, not a I-think-I'll-do-whatever-I-like place. That's called a playroom.

11. Esprit de Corps – a real trick. Probably results from clarity of purpose, attractiveness of vision, good communications, a coaching environment, a supportive performance culture and the open and swift resolution of dysfunction.

Seems like a reasonable foundation to me.

Fad alert...
Because of the elusiveness of effective management, it is susceptible to fad. Fads are not worthless, but they are often presented as the cure-all, the panacea. Therefore managers place too much faith in the miraculous ability of the fad to solve all their management dilemmas. Then, when disappointment sets in, managers totally reject the fad, throwing out the baby with the bathwater.

Some notable fads in my life time have been –

- One-minute management
- Total quality management
- Learning organisations
- Excellence
- Chaos
- Management by objectives
- Matrix management
- Process-re-engineering

They all had value, but were all presented as a new religion, which leads to cynicism (and the creation of a few millionaires, who I suspect are also cynical).

There is one exception...
...matrix management. This has no known value because, like time travel, it cannot be achieved. If you don't know what matrix management is, do NOT Google it – it will not enrich your life.

I do believe that good management is essential but rare. Good management is something you get better at as you get older. Good managers are NOT born. Management must be taught, seldom is and cannot be mastered in a classroom.

If you are a manager...
I salute you. Your job is hard. And essential.

In a Nutshell...
Good management usually leads to success and poor management usually leads to failure. Good management does not happen by accident.

How To Delegate

If you can delegate a task, delegate it. Delegation is essential to your personal productivity. And it helps the delegatee learn and grow, and they become more useful to you in the process.

Here's how to delegate...
1. Decide what it is you want to delegate.

It's best if you can continue to delegate the task on a permanent basis. Then you can make that task part of the delegate's job, and no longer part of yours. Also, leave your ego behind. You are NOT the only person in the world that can do the delegated task. And don't delegate horrible tasks. If you've got some horrible tasks, find a way to get rid of them.

2. Clarify the results you want.

Be specific and put a timescale on completion. Give the necessary resources. If appropriate, tell others what you've done so that if they normally assist you, they can now assist the delegate.

3. Delegate the result you want, not the method.

Give the delegate space to do things her way. It's a common mistake to delegate both the task and the method. This is suffocating.

4. Be patient.

The delegate will not be as skilled as you are straight away, but they will learn. Coach them. Trust them. Don't micromanage them.

5. Recognition.

Recognise them when the task is over and say thank you.

In my experience, people in organisations usually work at far too low a level. Almost everyone is capable of performing at a much higher level and would enjoy the chance to do so. It's your role as a manager to help your staff reach their potential.

With effective delegation, you can raise your game and your team's game – it's a win-win, and it's one of the major elements of effective personal and organisational productivity.

What can you delegate right now?

In a Nutshell...
Delegation takes courage but is a hugely powerful tool that empowers both the delegator and the delegate.

How To Empower People

OK but firstly, why bother?

You have two choices with people who work for you.

Choice 1
Empower your team. They will grow, become happier and more useful, allowing you to do bigger and better things, and in so doing you become happier and more useful too. It's a win-win. Everyone achieves more of their potential.

Choice 2
Don't empower your team. They will not grow, become less happy and less useful and will resent you because you have institutionalised them. You will not get the chance to do bigger and better things and you may develop an illusion of indispensability which is just another way of chaining yourself to your current role with no means of escape. It's a lose-lose.

I imagine you're finding Choice 1 a wee bit more appealing.

So, how to bring about this fabulous state of empowerment? There are a few things to think about...

Structure
Is the organisation set up to facilitate or hinder success? There's no point in being customer intimate if everyone works in silos with an internal focus. There's no point in pursuing a differentiation strategy and slashing the development budget.

Skills
The fact is that on-the-job training, whilst important, is often a very slow way to half-learn how to do something badly. Skills training and coaching is the fast-track to competence and through that confidence.

Systems
Internal and external. Get the critical business systems right so that people can work effectively and efficiently. Marketing systems that work; CRM systems that work. Accounting systems, key account management systems. It's endless. Almost everything is or should be seen as a system. This is not suffocating, it's liberating because it allows people to spend their time improving systems and giving more value through their creativity and initiative rather than re-inventing the wheel every day.

Managers
Make sure the bosses are not disempowering staff through control freakery, failure to delegate, and all the other crimes of the poorly training or badly managed manager.

Management is of course getting things done through other people. Management is not about setting yourself up as the charismatic mega-being; the only one who can do things; the indispensible super-achiever, surrounded by a team of barely sentient worker bees who, after training, might be able to carry your bags. I exaggerate to make a point, but I'm sure you might recognise this type of manager...

Joint Goal Setting
Staff should set their own goals. There needs to be iteration of course as some will play a game and some will genuinely underestimate their abilities, but let them take the lead. Then they have more ownership and motivation and a primal need to deliver what they said they would.

Delegate
The essence of management. People have jobs because tasks have been permanently delegated in the past. That's how organisations come into being and grow. From a people development point of view, delegation is like human growth hormone. How's that for an analogy!? I'm quite pleased with that one.

Share Information
Information is not power. Empowered teams with information is power.

Show Confidence
Show confidence in your team. Not wild "you can do anything" nonsense. More a quiet, positive, supportive "I can help you be even better".

So that's empowerment. An overused "buzzword" that is seldom unpicked and understood sufficiently to allow positive action can be taken.

Once you empower your team you become more empowered yourself. What goes around comes around. How good is that?

In a Nutshell...
Empowering people is a poorly understood buzzword. It's difficult to do well but it's worth doing well because the benefits are many. Empowering people is leadership.

DIY 360⁰ Feedback

I'm just back from hitting some golf balls in the gorgeous Ayrshire countryside. Ah Ayrshire...birthplace of Robert Burns.

"Oh wad some power the giftie gie us, to see oursels as ithers see us!"

He's clearly talking about **360⁰ FEEDBACK.** This is the process whereby your leadership skills are assessed by all those around you, not just your boss. So your team get a say. And your peers. And all your stakeholders.

It can be enervating but, for those who are big enough, enlightening.

What do you think they'd say about you? Because they're already saying it!

Don't be a timorous beastie.

In a Nutshell...
Actively seeking feedback on your performance from those you work with, both superiors and subordinates, is a very, very good idea, if you're big enough.

SPEED OF IMPLEMENTATION

The success of a venture, from the smallest marketing idea to an entire new business venture, depends on a lot of things, of course. One of them is speed of implementation.

Simply getting out there and doing whatever needs to be done quickly is of critical importance. There is only so much you can do mentally (all non-action is mental). You cannot plan-do-review if there's no doing.

So why do we sometimes implement so slowly, or even worse, not at all?

A number of reasons –
1. Knowledge Gaps.

Management is not about gaining total clarity before acting, it's about hitting the 80/20 sweet spot where 20% of the money and time that could be spent in preparation is spent yielding 80% of the achievable clarity. Then management is about execution, with a beady eye on the risks.

2. Perfectionism.

Waiting for the perfect moment to act. This is silly because there is no perfect moment.

However, there is the optimal moment. The moment when, allowing for the imperfections of life, conditions are propitious. Even sub-optimal may be OK. Sub-optimal does not mean "destined to fail". It just means things could be better but things can always be better.

3. Fear of Failure.

I believe there is no species on earth possessing the ability of us humans to talk ourselves out of action. What causes this fear?

It is, simply, *doubt*. Or *uncertainty*. We have doubt and uncertainty because we are intelligent. We see overwhelming confidence in others as naivety, or worse, stupidity. Our analytical brains cannot help but have doubt, to see the uncertainties.

So accept doubt for what it is – a marker of intelligence, and then use that intelligence to act anyway, despite the uncertainty.

The higher the speed of implementation the quicker you will be successful. Doing stuff gets results and results allow you to fine tune and get better results. Isn't it wonderful that we get better at something the more we do it? Wouldn't it be strange if this was not so?

It is also true that the higher the speed of implementation the quicker you will fail. This doesn't sound good but it is good. Not everything we do will work. If we implement quickly we will see failure coming earlier and then we can stop or change tack with minimal loss of money and time. The alternative is that we implement slowly and it takes years to find out what we have been doing isn't getting us to our destination. And the price of that is colossal, in money and, critically, time.

So, how to implement with real pace, with real speed?

Well of course there's all the usual management best practice that I bang on about all the time like getting everyone's motivation sorted out; planning - sufficiently detailed while avoiding perfectionism; setting goals and deadlines; defining your high-payoff activities and using blocktime to leverage this most precious of resources. I could go on.

These "outer game" tools and techniques are good.

But maybe there's a few elements of the "inner game" that need addressing –

Motivation – drill down really far into the "why"; the "reason for action". This requires real insight and honesty and rigour but when you crack it, it will power you straight through to your destination.

Learn to see doubt and uncertainty as your friends, without whom you would be very, very lost. They are signposts towards what risks we need to manage, not excuses for inaction.

Subjugate your ego – everything and I mean everything is secondary to the achievement of the goals. This means that you should get out of the way. Get off the critical path. Delegate and outsource until everyone's eyes water, and don't allow anything to be held up or delayed because someone is waiting for you to do something and you haven't got around to it. Don't worry – when you are successful everyone will know it was you in the driving seat.

In a Nutshell...
Speed of implementation is critical...the faster the better. Even if you fail.

WHAT YOUR STAFF REALLY NEED

What do your people really need from you? This has been researched many times over and the answers never really change.

Well, this is what they want:
1. You to show an interest in their career. That's right, their career. They want to know that in return for their exceptional efforts you will help them get to where they want to get to. After all, they're helping you to get to where you want to get to. Fair deal? I think so.

2. You are honest with them and they trust you. Honesty isn't just about not telling lies. It's about being fully open and in a timely manner. This is not just about the bigger business situation. It's also about dealing with their occasional poor performance immediately and effectively – not letting it fester until it's getting too late to do anything about it. Dishonesty includes truth avoidance and telling partial truths.

3. You have a vision of where you're going and how to get there and this is communicated well. It's about organisational purpose and direction. It's also about having a plan for teach staff member that shows that as a part of the organisation's journey to the sunlit uplands there is a plan to develop and improve each of them as well. There must be a win-win. "We're paying you to do the job" is not management or leadership.

4. You provide worthwhile work. Your staff need meaning in their jobs. Not all can have glamorous roles, but you must help them to see how their part plays a role in the journey to the sunlit uplands.

5. You recognise them. People need recognition. When they deserve it they need to receive it. Praise generates enthusiasm. Chastisement generates a sense of avoidance which leads to a sense of what the rules are which leads to a compliance mindset. An enthusiastic team versus a compliant team? Choose one.

In a Nutshell your people want to feel cared for, trusted, purposeful, worthwhile and recognised. That shouldn't be too difficult should it? They are human beings after all – not resource units.

Here's what they *don't* **ask for –**
Money – often a de-motivator in fact. Because they (and you) cannot win with money. There is always someone who got more and that sends a message that they are not as valuable as the person with more. It invites comparison with others and that's a game few can win.

Soft stuff – flexi-time, a gym, free canteen, marble foyer – never mentioned. I remember many years ago the CEO of ICI saying that "we're not in the crèche business". And this was in ICI, an organisation that elevated paternalism to a fetish. Well, he was right. We weren't in the crèche business.

The soft stuff is just fluff. It's nice, of course, but does it make someone feel better about a manager who doesn't care about their career, doesn't trust them, has no sense of direction, provides worthless work and offers no praise? Nope.

Remember what management actually is. It's the ability to get things done through other people. These other people have said what they want. Spending time, real time, on delivering the five points above is a critical management task and is time well spent. It's a high-payoff activity. Much better to do these simple things than spend time on useless nonsense; the ultimate useless nonsense of course being the need to deal with poor performance that has directly resulted from your inattention to the needs of your people.

Apart from the occasional bad apple, you get the staff you deserve.

In a Nutshell...

There's an unwritten contract between you and your best people. They help you in your career and you help them in theirs. Honour this contract and you won't have to wonder how to motivate them.

COMMUNICATION

"The Great Wall of China is the only man-made object that is visible from space" – memorable but not true.
Of all the skills of leadership, communication must be the most important. The absence of communication is unimaginable. Even silence sends a message. Lowly bacteria communicate – using chemicals.

Chip and Dan Heath have written a great book called "Made to Stick – why some ideas take hold and others come unstuck".

"The recommended daily allowance of iron for an adult is 14mg."
– true but not memorable.

They offer 6 key attributes that an idea must have to be effectively communicated.

First is...a focus on simplicity – "it's the economy, stupid" was dreamed up by an advisor during Clinton's presidential campaign to keep Clinton himself focused on the key issue.

Second is...to be unexpected – "if you haven't been in a car since 1965 the correct way to fasten your seat belt is...." as used by cabin staff on Southwest Airlines.

Third is...creation of a concrete image in the mind – how about this...

"If all the stars in the Milky Way were grains of salt they would fill an Olympic-sized swimming pool." – true and memorable.
Wow.

Fourth is...credibility – use statistics, but make them vivid!

"Only 37% of employees in the UK say they have a clear understanding of what their organisation is trying to achieve and why." "Only one in five was enthusiastic about their team's and their organisation's goals."

Yeah, so what? But if you re-frame it in terms of a football team...

"If this was a football team, only 4 of the 11 players would know which goal is theirs and only 2 of the 11 would care."
That's vivid!

Don't use statistics unless you're sure everyone understands!

Fifth is...be emotional – the Mother Teresa Effect

"If I look at the mass, I will never act. If I look at the one, I will."

Charities have long understood that talking about how your donation will help a named and pictured individual will generate over TWICE as much contribution as big picture statements on the awfulness of, for example, famine.

I don't think this is cynical...it's just about making it real.

So...is your message "real" - or are you just waving your hands about?

And finally...tell a story – we love stories because they allow us to relate to each other in ways we understand as fellow human beings. Think how well fables have endured.

In summing up...this is about communication so if you want your messages to be "sticky", make them...

- Simple
- Unexpected
- Concrete
- Credible
- Emotional
- ...and tell a story.

In a Nutshell...

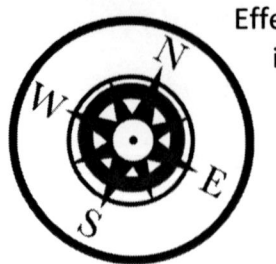

Effective communication to a generalist audience is hard.

MOTIVATING OTHERS

I am often asked; "how do I motivate my team." "How do I bring others with me?"

Well it's really easy, this is how you do it -

Share your vision. Describe a shiny, sunlit future where all is sweetness and light. Outline the part the person in front of you must play...they will swell with an abundance of motivation because they cannot fail to see the compelling future you have so beautifully painted. Group hug. The End

That's it.

Eh...no...
Unfortunately, you cannot motivate people effectively because, to them, you are an external force...

Kiss enough frogs...
"Sit down Kermit. I am extremely disappointed that, despite our repeated conversations around how it would be better for both you and this organisation if you were to become a prince, I cannot help but notice that you are still a bloody frog. What's wrong with you?"

You cannot motivate a frog to become a prince unless the frog is driven to want to be a prince and therefore doesn't really need external motivation.

The frogs that are capable of turning themselves into princes either have done so already or work tirelessly every day on their cunning plan to do so.

You can harness...
...their intrinsic motivation, but if it doesn't already exist within them you will struggle to create it.

By the way, there's nothing wrong with being a frog. We need frogs. They have a role.

But you can still make a difference...
You can demotivate frogs. Oh yes. This is easy. Here's how you do it - treat all the frogs the same, regardless of their potential. That's a good way to demotivate those with prince-potential. Or even better – promote a frog with no prince-potential so he's in charge of frogs with prince-potential – that's the quickest way I know to jettison any excess motivation you might have in your organisation. Try it (...if you haven't already.)

Motivation comes from within. It cannot be instilled. You can help someone to realise that they have huge potential, and you can work on their confidence, and their skills, but these are different issues.

Because motivation is...
...about attitude. The frog-princes know it. They feel it. They are intrinsically motivated. The good frogs who don't want to become princes are also intrinsically motivated, but not to become princes, and that's fine. I'm not having a go at good frogs.

All aboard...
Get the right frogs on the bus. You need some that have become princes, some with potential, and also lots of simply good frogs who are happy to be well-adjusted frogs. What you don't need are the frogs who bitch, moan and whine about the colour of the bus, how much the princes get paid, how their own prince-potential has been cruelly overlooked by every manager they've ever had...ya, ya, ya, ya...

Kick them out...
Sell them to the French. You cannot rehabilitate them. You cannot motivate them. They are toxic frogs and they do not improve with age. They fester. They have faulty thinking and you will not make the difference. You are not a social worker. Spend your time on the princes and the good frogs. Avoid at all costs the desire to rehabilitate

the problem frogs. 100% of all the motivation any frog will ever have is already within that frog.

In a Nutshell...

You cannot motivate anyone but demotivating them is easy. (Some) people can motivate themselves...treasure these people.

EMOTIONAL INTELLIGENCE

A bit longer than usual...but the same excellent quality...

IQ only gets you so far. Most of us have enough IQ points to do what we need to do. So what makes the difference?

There's nothing new under the sun...
Although the concept of "social intelligence" has been around since the 1920s, it wasn't until 1990 that the first scientific paper appeared on what was referred to as emotional intelligence. Then, Daniel Goleman wrote "Emotional Intelligence" in 1995, and things took-off. I've read it. It's not an easy read by any means. But it is a page turner, if you like that sort of thing, and I do.

Too much hype...
As is often the case, the usefulness of ideas like emotional intelligences has been obscured by all the shrieking headline-grabbing rubbish such as "only 20% of your success is due to IQ, the rest is due to EQ" (as emotional intelligence is often called, bizarrely). It's infinitely more nuanced than that.

We all know smart people who are difficult to deal with and could do better, if only they could fake being human. And we all know people who perhaps might struggle with an IQ test, but do very well thank you very much.

This is what the books say about the benefits of high EQ people...

Firstly...you just get them...
...people with high emotional intelligence are better at getting their ideas and goals across. They are more articulate, assertive and sensitive.

Secondly...great teams...

...emotional intelligence is closely associated with the skills required to operate effectively in a team.

Thirdly...bringing up baby...

...business leaders with high emotional intelligence build nurturing climates which increase organisational commitment, which in turn lead to success. (It has been reported that Fred Goodwin, the ex CEO of RBS, was authoritarian and cultivated a climate of fear in the corridors of his Edinburgh HQ. Authoritarianism is the antithesis of emotional Intelligence. I've never met him...he might be a real laugh...).

Fourthly...self-knowledge...

...leaders with high emotional intelligence are perceptive and know their own as well as their team's strengths and weaknesses, which enable them to leverage the former and compensate for the latter.

Fifth...I can cope...

...emotional intelligence is related to the coping skills which enable people to deal better with demands, pressures and stress.

Sixth...I know what you need...

...high emotional intelligence leaders can accurately identify what followers feel and need, as well as being more inspiring and supportive. They generate more excitement, enthusiasm and optimism.

Seventh...behave yourself..!

...managers with high emotional intelligence, unlike their low emotional intelligence companions, are less prone to negative, defensive and destructive coping mechanisms and decision making styles.

I can see success coming more easily to those with more of the above rather than less. I guess the key question is "can I improve my emotional intelligence and if so, how?"

Here's a start...
Well if emotional intelligence is all about understanding, managing and using emotions, which it is, because I looked it up for you after shouting at the kids to get off the computer, then you, like me, will agree that reflecting on the emotions you feel today, and what you allow them to do both to and for you, good and bad, is a step towards greater self-management and ultimately...leadership.

In a Nutshell...
Emotional intelligence contributes much more to success than IQ.

LEADERSHIP

Being a leader is easy.

There are many leadership models.

It's primal...
Daniel Goleman's is one of the best. He refers to six leadership styles in his book "Primal Leadership":

* The visionary leader inspires; believes in his own vision. Explains how and why people's efforts contribute towards the dream.
* The coaching leader helps people identify their own strengths and weaknesses and is a counsellor who encourages and delegates.
* The affiliative leader promotes harmony, is friendly and empathetic.
* The democratic leader is a superb listener, teamworker and collaborator.
* The pacesetting leader has a strong urge to achieve, lots of initiative, high personal standards, is impatient, micromanages and is numbers driven.
* The commanding leader says "do it because I say so"; is threatening, has tight control and drives away talent.

Best fit...
For any given situation there is a best fit leadership style.

The visionary leader is great when a radical change is needed. The coaching leader is just right when competent, motivated employees are available and performance improvement can be nurtured over the long term.

The affiliative leader works when there are rifts in the team, or great stress. The democratic leader is superb when consensus is required, and employee input sought.

The pacesetting leader is useful when the team is high performing already. The commanding leader is good in a grave crisis.

It's not all good...
Two of these styles are generally seen as having a negative impact on the broad organisational climate. Can you guess which two?

And the losers are...
Firstly, the pacesetting leader, because he requires followers of a strange disposition – they need to be competent, and motivated, yet require no empathy, no feeling of being involved and great resilience to micromanagement. This type of follower exists only rarely. If this leadership style is used exclusively, or poorly, as it often is, it is very negative on organisational climate. It is a style that is seldom necessary and never sufficient. I did have a pacesetting boss once. He was talented for sure. The experience was unpleasant (for us both).

Secondly, the commander, because he drives away talent. Nobody with any real individuality and self-esteem can work for someone who simply required their will to be carried out because it is their will. It doesn't work with kids, so why should it work with adults? This is the traditional military model of leadership. I used to work with an organisation that recruited ex-officers for their leadership capabilities. It never worked out. Never. Not once.

It's all about me...
My leadership style is coach. That's why I do what I do now. I like to think I have developed real vision for my own business, and that there's room for democracy and affiliation. I have no interest in pace setting and commanding.

We all have a preference for our individual leadership style. Sometimes we assume our comfortable preference must mean that that preference is appropriate, or right. That's a mistake. Comfort does not equal correct.

Do you feel me...?

And leadership isn't about you, it's about the situation, and how to generate resonance with the team. So they feel you. More than hear you...feel you.

It all comes easily to those with high emotional intelligence (which involves four abilities: self-awareness, self-management, social awareness and relationship management).

Sharpen your pencil...
And the great thing about emotional intelligence is that the four abilities are not innate, they are learned.

Leadership is situational – the right kind at the right time, to the right extent. You need to be the right leader for the situation. It's not so much about what each individual needs – that's more a management style issue, which I may write about next week.

The kicker...
I said at the start that being a leader is *easy*. But that's not leadership.

Being the right kind of leader at the right time is *hard*.
Unfortunately, that is leadership.

In a Nutshell...
The trick to leadership is being the right kind of leader at the right time.

TRUST

Merit trust...
Keep your promises to everyone. Especially loved ones, bosses, subordinates and children. I said everyone. And if you break a promise for reasons out of your control; explain, explain, explain. And bend over backwards to make it up to them. Never let a broken promise go unremarked, unresolved. But they should be very rare. Keep the promises you make to yourself as well. Don't disappoint yourself. It breeds laxity, and worse.

And in goal setting...
...don't call them goals. Call them promises. Try it, it works.

Don't lie...
Let's assume you're not a pathological liar. Let's assume you lie for the right reasons –

To avoid embarrassment...
...so you'd rather lie than be embarrassed? This is a self-esteem issue. If you've done something to be embarrassed about and it's got out the bag, you need to stand up in the glare and take it. Those around you will admire you, think more of you. Whereas to be caught lying, even over something trivial, especially over something trivial...

To avoid hurting others' feelings...
...most people would rather know the truth. Most, but not all. Frankly, someone who asks for your opinion wanting only one answer has put you in a no-win position and deserved all that they are just about to get.

To escape punishment...
...this is cowardice. Twenty years ago, I was in the back of a police car, in Hexham, having been stopped for over-exuberant driving, on an empty dual carriageway, late on a Sunday night. I already had more than my fair share of points on my licence, and if I got any

more I was taking the bus. Plus, I'd just accepted a new job in a new city, involving a lot of driving...

One of the policemen explained the technology that was used to ensnare me. I was familiar with it and said so. He turned to look at me and said:

"Are you a copper?"

Moment of truth time...

Say "yes" and maybe get let off? I'm not a bus person, I don't have the time. I've got this fabulous new job...I'm on a mission and the rules don't apply to me...I deserve this break, I am special, I really am!

It may seem trivial now. But it didn't at the time.

I said:

"No, I'm not a copper".

I took the bus, for 6 months. I took my medicine. It was foul. And it did me good.

Above, I said "Let's assume you lie for the right reasons". Trick statement! There are no right reasons.

We're all adults...

Now, I'm not suggesting that you lose the filter in your mind that stops your more unusual thoughts and feelings from being turned immediately into speech or emails. You must be diplomatic, and diplomacy is not about lying. Diplomacy is about understanding the impact you have on others and acting accordingly to minimise any unpleasantness. Minimise, not eliminate. We're all adults here.

Be trusting...

...give people the benefit of the doubt. I have done innumerable psychometric tests where I have been said to be overly trusting, or even naive. This is rubbish. I am neither. I would not let a stranger look after my children, my money or my home. I am not a fool. But I'll give new people my time, my attention, my focus. I will assume they will respond appropriately. And if they don't I have learned something about them.

But if I don't trust them...I am the loser.

To not give trust...to be overly guarded, suspicious, sceptical, defensive...is to never dare to taste a strawberry because it might be sour.

So what to do...
To be trustworthy and to offer trust are things that we can control. We have dominion over ourselves. We can choose to be and do these things. However, there is no guarantee that people will trust us, or merit our trust in them. But that's their loss.
Keep doing what you say and saying what you do; be consistent; be truthful; be transparent and open; offer trust to all; have faith in humanity. You will taste many more sweet strawberries than sour.

In a Nutshell...
Unless it is patently the wrong thing to do, we should trust people to do the right thing.

CULTURE

You manage the culture or it manages you.

It has been said so many times that culture is "the way we do things around here" that I cannot find an attribution.

But it's true.
In his 1992 book "Organisational Culture and Leadership" (I read these books so you don't have to), Edgard Schein describes culture as "a pattern of shared basic assumptions that a group learned as it solved its problems of external adaptation and internal integration, that has worked well enough to be considered valid and, therefore, to be taught to new members as the correct way to perceive, think and feel in relation to those problems."

Yup, that's about it.
He then defines three levels of culture:

Artefacts – those aspects (such as dress) which can be easily discerned but are hard to understand (and explains the idiocy of dress-down Friday).

Espoused values – conscious strategies, goals and values.

Basic underlying assumptions and values – this is the core or essence of culture. They are difficult to discern because they exist at a mostly unconscious level. But they provide the key to understanding why things happen in a particular way. These assumptions form around opinions on the deeper dimensions of human existence, such as the nature of humans, what is reality and what is truth.

It's the last one that's the killer. You can tell people they're now in the private sector, or they're now customer focused. You can train them until they're punch-drunk and set all the new objectives in the world, but until you change the basic underlying assumptions and values, it's all window dressing.

If you've had the misfortune to call British Telecom recently, you'll know what I mean. Or listen to a politician (underlying assumption of entitlement) or a journalist (underlying assumption that all politicians are corrupt).

I remember doing jury duty. It was clear to me that all the people in the court building who were paid to be there had an underlying assumption that everyone else was a criminal. And all the people who were not being paid to be there assumed the others were impotent and irrelevant. Both were right, and wrong. And it's when they're wrong that the bad stuff happens.

Ask yourself...
What are the underlying assumptions and values of your organisation? Are they truly helping your organisation to do what it needs to do? Your assumptions and values may be noble. They may be principled. You may be a lovely person. But that's not the point. Are your assumptions and values useful, or just comforting?

So what about your organisation...?
Terrence Deal and Allan Kennedy looked at two things: the speed at which organisations give feedback and reward to their employees regarding whether they are doing a good job or not, and the level of risk taking in the organisation. They came up with four types of organisational culture:

Another 2 x 2 matrix...
Tough-Guy Macho Culture (fast feedback and reward, high risk):

- Stress results from the high risk and the high potential decrease or increase of the reward.
- Focus on the present; individualism prevails over teamwork.
- Typical examples: advertising, financial brokerage, sports.

Work-Hard, Play-Hard Culture (fast feedback and reward, low risk):

- Stress results from quantity of work rather than uncertainty.

- Focus on high speed action and high levels of energy.
- Typical examples: sales, restaurants, software companies.

Process Culture (slow feedback and reward, low risk):

- Stress is generally low, but may come from internal politics and stupidity of the system.
- Focus on details and process excellence.
- Typical examples: bureaucracies, banks, insurance companies, public services.

Bet-Your-Company Culture (slow feedback and reward, high risk):

- Stress results from high risk and delay before knowing if actions have paid off.
- Focus on the long term, preparation and planning.
- Typical examples: pharmaceutical companies, aircraft manufacturers, oil prospecting companies.

So what to do...?
Ask yourself: what are my organisation's speed of feedback and reward (this should not really be a choice, it's the way it is, defined by the environment you operate in). What risks do you take? (Again, this is not a choice, not really, not if you're truly in the game). Do you have the right underlying assumptions and values? Do your colleagues? Staff?

Then define, create and maintain your culture to get the performance you desire. This is one of the most difficult and most essential management and leadership tasks there is.

But knuckle down, because you manage the culture or it manages you.

In a Nutshell...

Cultures bind people together and support (or hinder) goal achievement, so it's a good idea to create the right culture for you.

BEWARE OF GROUPTHINK!

Social psychologist Irving Janis coined the term "**groupthink**" to describe the situation where a group of people who have a high level of cohesiveness develop a desire to maintain unanimity that overrides their motivation to consider the facts of an issue in a realistic manner. In other words, they put "getting on with each other" above clear, objective thought.

There's more of it about that you think. Political parties and religious bodies are fertile grounds for groupthink, but no type of organisation is immune.

What are the symptoms of groupthink?

There is often an illusion of invulnerability – "we are special!" Also, there is often a belief in the inherent morality of the group – "we are right!" There is a very selective gathering of information – of course only that which accords with the group's view. And there is self-censorship – opinions are tempered and truth is discarded to maintain the group's cohesion. Finally, pressure is put on dissenters to "protect" the group from negative views.

So, what causes groupthink?

Well, as I mentioned, high levels of cohesion are involved. Also, the group tends to be insulated from any alternative opinions, either by design or through believing outside opinions are not necessary. Another key cause of groupthink is when there is a very directive leader who isn't shy at making her thoughts known.

Is groupthink bad...?

I'm afraid so. The group limits discussions to only a few alternatives. Ideas favoured by the majority will be quickly adopted without much thought for downsides or alternatives. Expert opinion is never sought. The group is highly selective in gathering information. There is high confidence in success and therefore there is seldom a Plan B....

So, how to prevent groupthink...?

Seek or be a devil's advocate. Encourage everyone to be a critical evaluator. The leader should keep her thoughts to herself. (I used to have a boss who would carefully outline his position on major issues before asking those around the table what they thought...ha!)

You can divide into subgroups or set up independent groups. Discuss issues with outsiders and invite others into the group to bring in fresh ideas.

And if you think this doesn't apply to you because you are self-employed I'm afraid it does. You don't need a group for groupthink, you can do it all by yourself in your own head....now there's a thought...

In a Nutshell...
Groupthink can result in a denial of reality. Beware.

How to Persuade People to Do What You Want

Ahh, skills of persuasion. A perennial favourite. How to get people to do what we want them to do. Well it can be tricky because adults are autonomous and self-directed and they won't do what you want just because you ask them, unless they like you, but that's not a strategy.

This takes me back to the old ICI competency handbook. Competencies have fallen out of fashion recently amongst the human resource fraternity, but that's just because they, like most people, like new shiny stuff every now and again. But for me, competencies are timeless, elegant classics. Like a gin martini...

So, what are these persuasion competencies? Well, there's three:

LOGIC
The first is rational persuasion or, as an ex-boss calls it - LOGIC.

Logic is all about building persuasive arguments based on logic, data and the merits of the situation. Great. Good start. Is this enough? Maybe. Probably not. A lot of rational, technical people never get beyond this because they believe that being "right" is all that matters. This is one of my favourite limiting beliefs. If logic was all that was needed, think how different the world would be. For a start, everyone would be like me. But they're not.

Here's something to do – check your assumptions. Regard them and those of others as things that need testing.

DIPLOMACY
The second competency is called strategic influencing, or DIPLOMACY (thanks ex-boss).

Diplomacy is all about being aware of the different forms and sources of influencing in choosing between different influencing strategies.

This is a subtle art indeed and I am not sure it is taught outside of the, er, diplomatic corps. Real diplomacy is rare – it is actual work and it takes time and patience.

Diplomacy is about lobbying key people, but it is also about considering a host of issues, like the politics of the situation, the cultures involved, what the personal relationships are and the importance of hierarchical positions.

Here's something to do – rehearse the way you wish to influence a situation, identify possible alternatives and then discuss them with someone who likes you.

EMPATHY
The third persuasion competence is called concern for impact, or as the same ex-boss calls it, EMPATHY.

Actively anticipating and responding to the feelings, needs and concerns of others. Your logical argument may offer the greatest good for the greatest number of people, but if it's my garden that's being turned into the high speed rail link, forgive me for not seeing your point of view. Now that's extreme and concern for impact is often more subtle.

Here's something to do – ask yourself what it might be costing others to agree with you and build their concerns into your proposals.

Take this a bit further – in agreeing with you and supporting you, what's in it for them? Nothing? No organisation ever did anything. People do stuff. And if can give them a personal win out of the decision you will be attractive.

I'm not talking underhand here – I'm talking about them getting something that is congruent with their self-image, their identity. If they want to be seen as innovative, make agreeing with you the innovative thing to do. If they want to be seen as offering security to their organisation, make your offer representative of security. If they are sufficiently senior to be turned on by courses of action that are transformational or dare I even say transcendent, and what you propose is these things, you have cracked it indeed. You are a master persuader.

Now this is all a bit of a performance and you won't want to take it to the n-th degree for the small stuff, but when there's big stuff at stake, it's worth spending the time.

Logic, diplomacy and empathy – it's usually takes all three to get what you want.

In a Nutshell...
There's three ways to persuade someone  of something. Best to use all three.

TEAMS

I've been working with a particular team performance model now for a few years. I have found it very effective, intuitive and easy to understand. It's by The Table Group.

Would you like more tea...
The thing about teams is that they often seem to be doing fine but really they're just being civil. You know, polite. But when they come under external threat, or have a significant, contentious issue to deal with, they very quickly fragment into factions.

This is because the team is not really built on sound foundations. The individuals can be superstars but teams are teams – they need a different kind of behaviour and this behaviour needs to be fostered.

Trust...
It starts with trust. What is trust? "I can trust you to be 10 minutes late!" That's not trust. That's predictability. Trust is about feeling able to be vulnerable in front of others. Being able to show weakness. And to know that the weakness won't be exploited. Now or in the future.

Conflict is good for you...
If a team trusts itself, then fear of conflict is diminished. This is important because conflict will almost certainly arise when major issues need to be addressed. These issues require full debate. If the team members fear the natural conflict that will arise and will not talk openly, then they cannot get to the next stage.

Yes, but, we didn't really consider...
No conflict (and its resolution)...no commitment. The team may well say they are committed, but when they are challenged by others outside of the team, they find it difficult to vigorously defend the decision if the natural conflicts within the team have not been resolved. This leads to a break down in cabinet responsibility and the projection of an image of fractured and inconsistent leadership. You see it all the time, particularly with politicians.

Dr Mark J Nugent

Commitment leads to accountability...
Once committed to a decision, people are more able to accept accountability and to hold their fellow team members to account. It is impossible to accept accountability where there is no commitment to the decision.

At last! What we're here for...
Without accountability, there is an inattention to results. And that's what the team's for. To get results.

Only at this level, with a trusting team, fully debating issues, building commitment and through that accountability, can all the team energy be focused on getting results. These teams are at the top of their game, but it doesn't happen by chance. It isn't some kind of interpersonal magic. It isn't something that happens in time, "once we get to know one another". That's just familiarity.

True team effectiveness is 2 + 2 = 5. Leaders make it happen.

In a Nutshell...
High team effectiveness is one of the best ways to gain competitive advantage.

THINKING

In the boardroom...
"I've got this great idea. It's a device you speak into and you can talk to other people who are far away. It'll allow us to speak to people in the next county!"

"But I don't know anyone in the next county."

"I know, but think how good it would be if you did!"

"But I don't..."

Kiss your comfort zone goodbye...
We develop habits of thinking. We become comfortable in our habits. And more certain of our correctness. We stifle creative thought. We suppress full and rational discussion and in so doing, miss the opportunity.

Edward de Bono is having none of it. The inventor of "lateral thinking" speaks of his Six Hats Thinking.

Put your hat on...
Choose a hat. You can wear many. And should.

White hat – think "neutrality".

A focus on information and facts. What's available and what can be found out. All the facts, not just the ones you like. No selective memory. No force-fitting. No post-event rationale.

Red Hat – think "fire!"

Emotions and feelings. "What do you feel about this?" No need to explain. Just state the feelings. Emotions are legitimate. They are not dirty secrets. It is said that women are, stereotypically, more emotional than men. And men make decisions based on objective rationality. This is, of course, poo. All decisions are emotional. It's just that men go through the post-event rational of thinking up good, "objective" reasons as to why their emotions are correct. And "objectivity" has a value in our society. Women tend to have moved on by this point.

Black Hat – think "judgemental".

Critical. Why it won't work. This is called "logical negative". Very common with technocrats with no vision. "Ooh, it'll never work." And those who are small and secretly think it's a great idea but only if it's their idea.

Yellow Hat – think "sunshine".

Optimism. It's all about benefits. What's good. This is called "logical positive". Sunshine and optimism – sounds flaky, doesn't it? You must be British. That's conditioning. Nothing wrong with sunshine and optimism. And remember, this is just one hat and you must wear them all.

Green Hat – think "vegetation".

Growth. Creative thinking. Possibilities. New ideas. Be a dreamer. But not only a dreamer. Why do we go to the moon – because it's there. Why do we map the human genome. Because we can, and who knows...

Blue Hat – think "sky".

Cool. Calm. Overview. Control of process. The chairperson ...organiser. Thinking about thinking. Someone has to. Otherwise it's a bun fight.

Know your enemy...
It's not about fighting a battle to see who's wearing the right hat. It's about wearing all the hats, and fighting a battle against our comfort zones, to solve the problem, or realise the opportunity.

It's about removing the barrier that is our individual ego. That puts us before the problem or the opportunity.

Don't get me wrong – ego is great. Without it we'd be pond life. But it's a double edged sword. To be used, with caution. Make ego–gratification equal to solving the problem or realising the opportunity, not "winning" a fight with your colleagues.

Here's how to do it...
Get a facilitator to do white hat, blue hat and manage the process.

Then challenge people.

"Yes I know you can see how this will not work." "And we welcome that" (We really do – a sceptic is usually worth their weight in gold.)

"But we ask more of you. We ask you to contribute more fully. To think about what might be; how we can make it happen; how good it could be."

Then we'll make a decision. Based on a full and open discussion. Not on who has the greatest ability to argue. My wife sometimes says to me "you haven't won the argument, you're just better at arguing."

She has a point.

And the lesson is...
That the objective needs to be met to arrive smiling at the best result for the issue at hand.

No ego is required.

The six hats are required.

Try this...it works.

In a Nutshell...
We tend to get fixed in our ways of thinking.
This is limiting. The "Six Hats" is the answer.

Zero Tolerance of Poor Performance

People are our greatest asset. Yeah, except the ones who are liabilities.

He's great...
The discretionary effort of people is what fuels companies. Not the contracted hours, not the bloody job description. It's the sweat they put in when they are not really being paid. The diligence; the applied intelligence; the additional contribution. Over and above the call of duty. When they are motivated, turned on, inspired and driven. When they have a superb attitude. Not always super-skilled or experienced. But with a great attitude. These people are assets.

But sometimes so cruel...
On the other hand, we have the moaners and whiners. You will have one, maybe more. Think of them now. Somewhere along the line it went wrong. Maybe it went wrong before they joined. They suck up management energy. They suck up their colleague's energy. They cast a pall. They have externalised their plight. It is someone else's fault – the boss, the management, the fact that every boss they've ever had has failed to recognise their potential. These people are liabilities.

I can change him...!
I have worked in companies where we have tried to bring these people back into the fold. To turn liabilities into assets. They have been lavished with attention – from HR; from their manager; from their manager's manager. Maybe some have been sent on courses. Plans have been written. Our fundamental faith in human nature tells us that, this time, this time, we will convert the liability into an asset.

I have watched this for 20 years. I have been as caught up in the "this time it'll work" delusion as anyone else. Because I am an optimist. Maybe even an idealist. Sorry about that.

Nothing I say makes any difference...!

But it never has worked. The liabilities do not become assets. They never change. In my experience, it is worse than that. They atrophy. They see the time and money lavished on them as vindication of their victimhood. "Look at all this attention I'm getting. They have finally woken up to how badly I have been treated by every boss I've ever had."

This is killing me...
I believe that many companies are destroyed by their people. Or at best hidebound, hamstrung and left to fester in the wastelands of zero-growth living dead companies like so many zombies in a schlock movie. They're not zombified by exchange rates, or inflation, or macroeconomic factors, or bad products or theft. They are slowly strangled by liability people who hit the company in three ways – by being unproductive in the first place and therefore just a cost; by dragging the assets down; by consuming management time and thereby leaving less of it for the asset people and the good projects that will take the company forward.

I can't take it anymore...
There's a tipping point. When the level of liability people swamps the organisation. It's at different points for different organisations. But for all of them it's very much lower than 50%. I would guess it's about 20%. One in five.

It's just not working out...
Simplistically, at Tolerance Ltd, where one in five of the people are liabilities, your people costs are 25% higher than the competition (four working, five being paid). At Tolerance Ltd, the management are only 80% as effective as the competition (20% of time being spent on the liability). Further, at Tolerance Ltd, the four asset employees begin to go off the boil because the liability is not being dealt with. They carry him. And they are sick of it. Because it is not fair. And their discretionary effort is applied less often and with less effect. In time, they are still good people, but their edge has been dulled by the liability.

I can do better...

Meanwhile, at Zero Tolerance Ltd, things are different. They love people. They understand they make the difference. And because they understand this they identify liability people very quickly and take immediate steps to understand why this is. If the liabilities can be fixed, they get fixed. If not, management manage that person out of the organisation. They do this not because they are heartless capitalists, but because they love the asset people, and to allow these people to work in the presence of the toxic few is a crime.

Assets are only happily matched with liabilities on a balance sheet. With people, one destroys the other. Have zero tolerance for liability people.

In a Nutshell...

Most people are assets. A few are liabilities. For the sake of the assets, the liabilities need to be improved or removed.

How to Listen

LISTEN TO ME! I found myself screaming at someone the other day. It was amazing – everything I said to him seemed to steer him right back to what he wanted to talk about. I was simply the guy on the other end of their conversation. If I'd been replaced by someone else, he'd have said the same things. Like a two-way radio stuck on transmit only.

And they were trying to sell me something!

Yak Yak Yak.

Hysterically, this person finished my sentences for me, but in so doing revealed that he didn't know what I was going to say...!

He probably thought he had the gift of the gab. He's probably been told that. And thought it was a compliment. The thing about the gift of the gab is it isn't a gift. It's a pain in the neck for those who have to listen to this type of market stall drivel.

So I screamed at him LISTEN TO ME. But I'm reasonably well behaved these days so I only screamed at him in my head. If he had listened to me, he might have made the sale. I actually wanted what he was selling. But I was not going to reward him – I'll reward someone else who has similar stuff but actually listens.

So, how to listen?
It's not that hard, but like everything else, you need to want to do it. You need to understand that really listening is the right way to behave, and not just when you're selling. No degree of discipline and technique-honing will make you a good listener if your real reason for doing it is as a sneaky tool to get what you want.

So, what to do?

Firstly, listen attentively without interrupting. Don't finish people's sentences for them. Maintain eye contact. They are trying to communicate with you, so let them do it.

Secondly, when they stop talking, pause before replying. Don't just rush in. Don't be afraid of a second or two of silence. And if you've been formulating your brilliant repost while they've been talking and are waiting for a microsecond's break to launch your sparkling reply into the conversation like a cruise missile, go back to the first step.

Thirdly, seek clarification. "What do you mean by...?" "Explain that to me again..." Get their message: loud, clear and accurate.

Fourthly, play back what's been said to you; allow the other person to correct you or confirm you've got it right.

That's listening – attention, pause, clarify, repeat. It's not linear, you can skip around.

Two things happen when you listen properly.

One - you actually understand better, which is calming.

Two - you've been respectful and they'll like you for that. We all need to be understood. You will stand out as someone who seeks to understand.

As I said, you cannot do this as a manipulative technique, so if that's where you are – don't waste your time.

But if you do actually wish to understand your fellow human being as we career through this life...give these simple techniques a try. Take the time.

In a Nutshell...

When someone speaks to you, listen to them. Conversation is not a battle to be won.

WHAT TO DO IN MEETINGS

I have spent probably far too much of my life in meetings. It's very much how we live in organisations. Whether it's a client meeting, a supplier meeting or an internal meeting (which come in many flavours: one-to-one, small groups, large groups, one hour, one day, three day conference with 300 people). We spend a lot of time doing this.

It's essential – teams do more than individuals ever can. But the opportunities for massive time wasting, partial brain atrophy and pins and needles in the bum are legion. Plus all that bad food. Don't these people know sausage rolls should be WARM.

So, how to make sure you always have a worthwhile meeting?

Firstly, define what it is you want to learn. Maybe it's an update from a colleague, or a subordinate. Maybe it's understanding a new piece of technology in your marketplace. Or how the competitors are getting on. How the boss feels about something. Or a chance to get to someone who is hard to get to.

If there is not sufficient learning to be had from the meeting that merits the time involved don't go, or go for a portion of the meeting.

Secondly, be clear on what you will contribute. And then contribute it. At the right time. And in the right forum. A few concise, well-crafted words at the right time will stand you apart from the hesitators, repeaters and deviators that come out of the woodwork for most meetings.

Again, if you cannot contribute, ask yourself if you should be going to the meeting at all.

Thirdly, if you do go to the meeting, make sure there is an output, an action plan. Learning and contributing are good, but these need to lead to action – for you and those you interact with. There needs to be a new course of action coming out of the meeting.

Consider the three elements above in the context of your agenda. That's right – **your** agenda. The meeting organiser may have her own agenda, but you don't need to play. Certainly you must not be disruptive, or try to take over, unless you are the boss and a bad one at that. More subtly, simply prosecute your own agenda quietly but with purpose. No one else need know you came to the meeting with your own list of objectives.

And the bigger and longer the meeting the better. Because the meeting is the whole event – including the breaks, lunch, maybe dinner and the bar afterwards if it's that sort of do.

What will you learn? Maybe from a coffee break chat with a targeted individual?

What will you contribute? Your contribution doesn't have to be in open forum in front of everyone. It could be a well-honed viewpoint given to a more senior person, again, maybe at lunch. Avoid talking for talking's sake. Choose your targets.

What actions do you want others to leave with? Pretty much depends on your contribution. Is it compelling enough to merit action? How good are your influencing skills? Are you approaching your target in the right way?

It is quite possible that 299 people out of the 300 that attend a three day conference on the blue widget market at an airport hotel in Nordwestupperholtensteinburg will leave feeling frustrated and bored.

But not you
If you have learned what you set out to learn, contributed well and appropriately, and have a few actions in place with key people, you will probably have been the most productive person there. You will

not feel frustrated and bored. You will have made progress. And the numb bum will wear off, eventually.

In a Nutshell...

Meetings can be a lot more fun and a lot more useful if you proactively pursue your own agenda.

How To Have A Senior Team Meeting

Call it what you will – Leadership Team, Business Team, Steering Team. You name it.

If there's two or more of you in your organisation, division, department etc., you need to be having a regular meeting to manage and lead.

That's what you're there for, right?

Here's what to do –
1. Meet for at least one day, and preferably two days, every quarter, or better still every two months. Get out of the office. Stay over at least for one night. Have dinner and drinks. You are in a senior position and you need the time to be a team. This is not a luxury. It is a necessity. Yes, it costs money, but not nearly as much as it costs when you don't have these meetings. That costs real money.

2. Have a standing agenda. It might look like this –

- Review minutes and actions of last meeting – led by Boss, 30 minutes.

You need to agree that the minutes are a fair reflection of what went on. Then you review the actions agreed at the meeting. Failure to complete an action should be such a rarity that when it does occur it's actually slightly shocking. And the failure should not be a surprise to the boss, as the reason for failure should have been communicated to the boss beforehand. The reason must be genuine - things may have changed, it may not have been possible to achieve the goal for external reasons. Maybe something else has to happen first. These are good reasons.

"I didn't get round to it" or "I've been really busy" are bad reasons. They are thinly veiled code for "I don't respect my colleagues or my boss. I make promises that I don't keep. I cannot manage myself and I suspect I'm probably not really a senior manager."

- Operational Review – led by Operations Managers – 60 minutes each.

Operations are what turn your strategy into results. So you may have a few operations that matter – marketing, selling, R&D, various projects, manufacturing, logistics etc. This part of the meeting is, in the case of manufacturing, about how many blue widgets you said you'd make, how many you made, an explanation of the difference if there is one, and a heads up on any looming issues.

- Strategic Issues – led by X – 2 hours

You may need to discuss something strategic. For example, a capital expenditure proposal. Or a change to strategy. Or a competitive issue. Or just some great idea you've had.

- HR Issues – led by X - 60 minutes.

Take some time out to discuss those pesky people that work in the organisation. How's the management development programme coming along? Who's a star? Who's struggling? Who needs a free transfer to Accrington Stanley?

- Any Other Business (AOB)

Like it says – anything else you need to discuss.

Also, notice each agenda item has a nominated lead and a time slot.

3. The boss should get the agenda out two weeks beforehand. Some agenda items, e.g. the strategic issues, may merit a pre-meeting paper to be written and circulated. The boss should make this clear when the agenda is circulated and the papers should be made available by the nominated author at least one week before the meeting.

4. During the meeting, have a scribe – someone to take the minutes. This is not onerous. It's a brief note of key points, decisions and actions (what is to be done, by whom, by when). Minutes should be circulated within 24 hours of the meeting closing.

5. These Senior Team meetings should be scheduled 12 months in advance. They are NEVER cancelled. EVER. If you're on the senior team you attend. You do NOT take your holiday when a Senior Team Meeting is scheduled unless you are either a) psychotically passive-aggressive and/or b) this is your non-verbal way of saying "I want out".

These meetings are mission critical. The Senior Team steers the ship. Does the thinking. Takes the plaudits. And the rap. It's leadership at the end of the day.

We're talking about maybe eight days a year. Three to four percent of the working days. In this time your team will develop the trust it needs. You will get over your fear of conflict so that you can genuinely commit to action and accept real accountability for your actions. Then, and only then, will you really perform.

In a Nutshell...
If you value management you will take the time and the space to have effective senior team meetings. They are not a luxury.

THE KEY TO NEGOTIATION

I was 27 years old when I took off my lab coat for the last time. I was to become a buyer, then a sales rep, then a marketing guy, then a sales manager...and so on.

I had to negotiate.

For the first time.

Hmmm...negotiate. Sounded scary. Somewhat different to test tubes, chemicals and the certainty of the lab.

Negotiation isn't really what a lot of people think it is. It isn't win-lose. It isn't personal. It isn't a battle. It isn't about slick tricks and techniques. Or rather it doesn't have to be.

It is about preparedness, thoughtfulness and suppressing your own ego.

There are many keys to negotiation, not just one.

There's understanding who you're dealing with – are they the decision maker (there is only one you know, the person who can say "yes" and they don't wear a badge). Or are you talking to one of the many people who cannot say "yes", but can say "no"? (In that the decision maker will not say "yes" if this trusted colleague is saying "no").

Another key is having many options for getting to an agreement – the more options you have, the better your chance of getting agreement. It is tempting to construct in your head the perfect outcome, convince yourself it is fair to all parties and go into the meeting with your shiny solution. But unless you're very lucky the other guy probably does not share your view of the perfect outcome. So generate options, options, options.

Yet another key to negotiation is to focus on interests, not positions. What interests are shared by the parties in the negotiation? Common interests will lead to a solution. Focusing on moving the other guy from his position while largely keeping yours unchanged isn't going to work.

In *Getting to Yes: Negotiating Agreement Without Giving In,* Roger Fisher and William Ury describe one key to negotiation you MUST have...

Your **BATNA**.

You need a **BATNA**. Your **Best Alternative To a Negotiated Agreement**. Your Plan B as it were. When you have a BATNA, your objective for the negotiation is to better your BATNA – to come up with an improvement. This is a low risk objective. If you fail...so what? You've got a Plan B.

But if you have no BATNA, your objective in any negotiation is to do a deal... any deal. This is not a good place to be psychologically. It breeds fear, anxiety and meekness. And those show.

You see this on Dragon's Den – the hapless entrepreneur offers 20% of their company for £50K. They get a single offer of £50K for 40% of their company. All they can do here is accept or walk away. (Interestingly, when they walk away it is seldom because they have a BATNA, it's because they cannot stomach "giving away" so much at an emotional level).

They cannot negotiate because they have no BATNA. They must accept or decline. Yet they try to negotiate. And they do it meekly. They question "will you accept 30% for the £50K?" It's never a statement: "I'll give you 30% for the £50K". It's always a question. I have to look away at this point. The answer from the Dragon is always "no" and it should always be "no". Then the hapless entrepreneur accepts at 40% anyway but there's one difference – they've blown their credibility and they've begun a new relationship having diminished themselves because they've asked for something, not received it and accepted the fact that they've not received it.

It's OK to do this in one-off transactional negotiation, e.g. buying a washing machine where you're not trying to build a relationship with the other guy or establish credibility. But if you plan on meeting the other guy again across the negotiating table or the boardroom table, you need credibility and trying to negotiate without a BATNA is the quickest way there is to destroy your credibility.

Get a BATNA. It changes the game.

In a Nutshell...
In negotiation, without a BATNA you are probably dead meat.

PART 3
MASTERING YOUR MINDSET – THE USER'S GUIDE FOR YOUR BRAIN

Mindset Matters

Purpose

Self-Efficacy

Easy as ABC

How to be Resilient

Are You Assertive?

Stop Thinking About That

Present and Correct?

9/11, Resilience and You

When it's Good to Externalise

Excellence

The First 60 Minutes Really Matter

How to Do Anything

The Seven Habits Still Ring True

Sharpen the Saw

I Love Failure and You Should Too

Dr Mark J Nugent

Free Will

Limiting Beliefs

Attitude

Values

Failure

Being Aware

Motivation

How to Stay Positive

The productive application of our knowledge, as covered in Parts 1 and 2 can take us far but there will be a limit. The limit is usually within us. It is our mindset. At the top level of professional sport, this is well understood. The business world and the educational world have some way to go to catch up.

This is the most important part of this book. The brain is the most complex thing in the universe. Yet we have not been issued with a user guide. I have tried to put together for you some useful ideas that will allow you to maximise the ways in which your brain can help you and to be alert to the ways in which your brain can hinder you.

Get this mindset stuff right and you will feel totally in control, motivated, positive and focused. This will really help you to achieve what you want to achieve. And when you really begin to focus on your mindset and take steps to improve what that can do for you, you will discover an interesting side-effect: you will be happier. Try this. It works.

MINDSET MATTERS

I might be a bit behind the curve here, but I've just realised something. When getting stuff done, having the greatest tools and processes is fine but if you don't use them you might as well not have them. And to use them you need to be in control of your mind. The mental game is paramount.

Achievement, at any level, is about the methodology *AND* mindset. I guess my realisation is not so much about the importance of mindset but is about the fact that although we understand the importance of mindset we still do so very little about it.

Education seldom addresses it. Most coaches barely touch on it. Why?

Because it's hard? Because it's a bit wooo-wooo?

But it's half the game, and probably more.

If I was presented with a choice between –

1. Having the best tools and processes in the world but seldom using them because of some mental barrier like procrastination, and

2. Having good enough tools but a mindset that not only didn't hinder me but helped me...

I'd go for the latter every time. Who wouldn't?

There will always be a need for better tools and processes but I think most of that stuff is readily available and of high quality:

- Sales as a process is understood (transactional and consultative)
- Marketing is understood
- Operational excellence is understood
- Strategic planning as a process is understood

It's all available. You may not have it in your head but you can get the overview for nothing from Google and if you want the complete toolbox someone will sell it to you.

But distinction in performance comes from mastering the mental game.

The sports people have known this for ages.

There's two levels to this –

First level – throw out the rubbish...
When not fully commanded by you, your mind has a tendency to produce rubbish: procrastination, fear, negative self-talk, biases, prejudices, bad beliefs, tribalism, being a slave to emotions – and that's just me...

I cannot take each of these apart in a 600 word article. Suffice to say, it's all rubbish and none of it has a place in anyone's head.

Second level – putting your mind to good use...
Taking charge – *you* being aware of everything that your mind injects into your consciousness and *you* deciding whether or not to keep the thought. If the thought doesn't serve you, reject it pretty quickly.

- Taking the time to consider what's possible and seeing all barriers as temporary and surmountable. In other words, thinking BIG. Genuinely believing that the sky is, in fact, the limit.
- Realising you have free will and actually using it.
- Constantly pushing your comfort zone.
- Learning continuously. (Really – if we are not learning what are we doing?)

Once again, the sports people are showing us the way. Top athletes these days have physios and coaches of course but they also have head doctors as well. Because once the 10,000 hours of training has been done (4 hours a day 5 days a week for a decade) and the body has reached its potential, the mind will make you or break you. The mind will either make you transcendent, or will trip you up on the final lap.

I am not sure why we neglect the mindset issue. Maybe it's because education is, rightly, at least for a while, tools-based. We need the three Rs. But to keep going solely on the tools-track is robotic. As we mature and the normal stuff becomes routine, we need to look further afield for development. We need to look at our mindset.

We need to think more like top athletes (but without the 10,000 hours of slog).

And this is good because mindset is within our sphere of control. Looking for a new tool..."I need a better spanner"... is pretty close to a workman blaming his tools. It's an *externalisation*. This is never good.

But "I'm going to master the inner game of mindset" sounds like something we can actually do. We might not know how but we'll work it out.

And this is an *internalisation* which is...

a) better than an *externalisation*...

and...

b) the first step to self-mastery...

In a Nutshell...

Without a helpful mindset, the tools and techniques for improvement will never provide an enduring and positive change.

PURPOSE

Ideal Homes...
The benefits of having a purpose are clearly demonstrated by my children. When they are purposeful they are quiet (sometimes), resourceful, diligent, hardworking, have the goal in mind and co-operate freely. They achieve their desired result and they are happy and rightly proud of what they have done. Their confidence soars.

Towerblock...
When they have no purpose, they are listless, snappy, irritable, complaining and bad tempered. They goad each other, get increasingly frustrated and are unproductive. Their mental state is poor (and deteriorates). They achieve very little and they are not happy. Their confidence dives.

Just like adult life, only starker because children don't wear masks.

You gotta have a purpose...
Your business needs to have a purpose, or as it is unhelpfully called, a Mission Statement. It really should be called a Purpose Statement because no one would admit to not having a purpose, or their purpose not being in the forefront of their mind.

Your Purpose Statement should be desirable to you and those who work with you. Feelings toward it should be the number one interview question asked of prospective employees.

The Purpose Statement should be displayed prominently, understood and acted upon by all, and seen as an important and useful strategic tool in your business (even if it's just you in your business).

This place is knocking me out...
But don't fret if your Purpose Statement is a bit rubbish, or non-existent.

Opportunity knocks...

You have an excellent opportunity. Get your people together or have a meeting with yourself, and define your Purpose Statement. This will give you direction, aid decision making and the key goals will identify themselves. You will have a shared purpose and when you have a shared purpose you'll be ahead of the game and that's what leadership is about.

In a Nutshell...

Your purpose derives motivation. Express it clearly. Then communicate widely.

SELF-EFFICACY

I've been re-reading **Putting Out of Your Mind** by Bob Rotella. He's a sports psychologist for golfers. A head doctor if you will. He walked the Open Course with Darren Clarke in 2010 and is seen as a major contributor to Clarke's victory that year.

In this book he suggests that, when lining up a put, we believe with all our being that the put will drop into the hole. We visualise it. We tell ourselves it will happen. We see it so clearly it is as if it has already happened. AND, we don't care if we miss.

It's basically about what psychologists call self-efficacy. Very crudely, self-efficacy is our belief about how effective we are at doing something. How skilled we are. How competent.

The key word is belief. Our belief about how effective we are, or could be.

Many studies have shown that it is better to have an inflated belief of your abilities than a deflated one. Yes indeed, confidence, even over-confidence is good, if annoying for those around you.

Self-efficacy is important because it affects almost everything we do. The more self-efficacy we feel about a task or challenge, the harder we work at it. That's another wee quirk of the human mind. We work harder at the stuff we think we can do.

Critically, I think the better we think we could be in the future, if we apply ourselves, is also a part of self-efficacy. The acceptance that we might be a bit rubbish at the start but having a belief, from self-knowledge, that we could get better in the future – that's also self-efficacy. The books don't mention this "self-efficacy orientation," and I just made it up, but it rings true to me.

Taken to extremes in the other direction, the poorer we think we are at something, the less hard we try, until we give up entirely.

Psychologists have a name for this too. It's called learned helplessness. Isn't that dreadful – learned helplessness? Ugh.

There are two staircases here.

On the first staircase we take action. We improve. We gain competence and hence confidence and so we take more action and so it goes on. It's an upwards staircase to the top floor where there is a glass ceiling below an azure blue sky. This is self-efficacy. Psychologists actually say that this is the route to a happy and productive life. They really do. I have the book in front of me (**Understand Psychology** – Nicky Hayes).

On the second staircase, we seldom take action and when we do take action we are hesitant. Failure or poor results are immediately seen as evidence of our lack of competence. We pull back, do not improve and our competence and hence confidence does not rise. Eventually we stop. Further attempts at action become less and less frequent. We have attained learned helplessness. This is the staircase down into the basement. Where there is no light. We are doomed. Death soon follows.

OK. OK. I'm joking about the death bit.

I had a brush with self-efficacy recently (actually all the time but this is a neat wee example). I put together a significant website for one of my coaching programmes. It took about two weeks. It was a lot of work. Most of it outside of my competence. I had so much to learn. I had to do some videoing of me, of all people. Here's me not yet with the physique of the Tour de France rider and some say a face for radio. Then I had to deal with masses of technology – editing, screen recording...and then the wonder of third party video hosting in the cloud (wot?). It was quite stressful at times and the children were shouted at on more than one occasion (poor self-control). And there were times when I put my foot on the first step of the staircase to the basement...

For example when after two days of video editing I discovered that all my videos were stuttering like Max Headroom (remember him?). But I knew I was going to sink the put. I knew I could do it because, hey, if it can be done by anyone I can do it too. That's my self-efficacy orientation kicking in. I knew that we as humans have this really funny characteristic where when we do things we seem to get better at them! And in fact, to turn it around, if we don't do things we CANNOT get better. And the converse of getting better is that in the past we were less good, or rubbish. (I used to have a boss once in my early career who at annual appraisal time would look at my improvement over the year and criticise me for being more rubbish at the start! The only way to avoid this criticism would be to never improve! I guess management just isn't for some people.)

So where am I now? Well, the video website is up and running and a critical skill set I need for the future has been developed (first steps at least).

What seemed like a huge black hole of zero competence now holds no fear for me. I have improved my self-efficacy massively in an important area and I look forward to my next video/web project not with helplessness but with enthusiasm. I am on the right staircase.

In a Nutshell...
If you think you can, you can. And the converse applies also.

EASY AS ABC

Or...there's two ways to think - one for winners and one for er...non-winners.

Someone dared to doubt me the other day. Can you believe it? I was banging on about how we can control what we think about and how that, in turn, controls what we do, i.e. our behaviour and, in turn, how our behaviour generates the results we get, good or bad.

This person wasn't buying it. No, no. There was no linkage between the mental and the physical, he said. It's all luck anyway. You're talking mumbo-jumbo. Hmm...

This reminded of someone...
...I met fleetingly at a conference. She had the following philosophy – "I never expect anything good to happen. Then I won't be disappointed." I may have written about her before. Do you think she's right? Do you think that never expecting anything good to happen has no effect on her behaviour and hence her results? Of course not. She won't strive for the good stuff because she cannot risk disappointment. So good stuff never happens.

She wasn't easily mistaken for a ray of sunshine, I can tell you.

The poor woman...
...has an unhealthy belief. She believes she has to protect herself from disappointment by having low expectations of what will happen in her life. She has very little or no tolerance for disappointment.

How do we unravel this? Well, psychologists have a three box model for this. It's called "ABC". Business consultants usually have a four box model for things, with a fancy name. That's why they're paid more.

Back to psychologists...
So what's this "ABC" malarkey?

A stands for some sort of trigger event.

B stands for beliefs – healthy or unhealthy.

C stands for consequence – thoughts, emotions, actions and symptoms.

And it's sequential – A leads to B which leads to C. Then it loops round again. And again.

Now, I don't know…
…what this woman's trigger events were, but the C for consequences is clear: unhealthy thinking, low expectation, insufficient action and poor results.

Now I am not saying that beliefs need to be synthetically positive. I am saying that when we have a naturally negative belief, i.e. making a four hour presentation to 800 people is scary, that we make the belief healthy/negative, rather than unhealthy/negative.

The good…
So we might think "I am really nervous about this presentation but that's normal and I can function despite feeling that way." That recognises the reality and will lead to a more positive result.

The bad…
Here's the unhealthy/negative version – "I am really nervous about this presentation. I hate feeling that way. I can't bear it." That does not recognise the reality (can't bear it – really?) and will get a poor result.

In the case of the woman I met at the conference – she's thinking "I cannot tolerate disappointment. When I am disappointed it is awful. It is horrible. I cannot bear it." This is an unhealthy/negative belief.

Here's the converse – "I accept that sometimes I will be disappointed. I don't want to be but it will happen. That's life and my worth does not depend on being free of disappointment." That's healthy/negative.

Simple but important...
Now this is an extreme and simple example, but the C – the consequences that derive from each of these B's are polar opposites.

There is nothing wrong with negative beliefs – all goal achievement that involves change, i.e. all worthwhile goal achievement, has discomfort associated with it and we cannot help but feel negative emotions about that. And that's OK. It's not about eliminating the negative; it's about making the negative healthy.

Here's some healthy vs unhealthy examples –
"Want to" vs "Have to"...

Wanting to do something is about choice. Having to is usually about fear. Choice is better. "I am going to study because I want to pass this exam" is good. "I have to do this stupid studying because I must pass this exam" is rubbish.

"Bad" vs "Awful"...
Things can often be bad. They are seldom truly awful.

"Difficult" vs "Unbearable"...
Making those phone calls may be difficult. The activity is NOT unbearable. Get a grip.

"Self-acceptance" vs "Self-damning"...
Sh*t happens. It doesn't make you a sh*t.

Getting this stuff right is really important in goal achievement. Unhealthy/negative beliefs are like poison to achievement. They are inflexible, inconsistent with reality and unhelpful. They lead to self-sabotage.

Healthy/negative beliefs are what balanced grown-ups have. They are flexible, consistent with reality and hugely helpful.

Getting this right is not just about goal achievement, it's one of the cornerstones of being happy. So be happy.

In a Nutshell...
How you think, what you feel and what you do are entirely up to you. Many people find this hard to accept. They are wrong.

HOW TO BE RESILIENT

One of the differentiating characteristics of high performers is the way they react to setbacks and failures. This is important because setbacks and failures will and should happen as the only sure way to avoid them is to stay so far inside your comfort zone that you achieve nothing anyway and that in itself is a failure – a failure to act.

Setbacks and failures mean we are pushing ahead and they are signposts on the road to victory but they are seldom seen as such. Therefore we will only make progress if we learn to deal with setbacks and failures effectively and not let them become barriers to future action.

There are only four positive things to do when a setbacks or failure occurs. They are not mutually exclusive – you can do more than one of them. In fact, you can do them all, and you should.

1. Learn
Objectively assess what went wrong. Be easy on yourself. Remember – failure is just a result you didn't want. It's not a judgement on you personally. What have you learned? Take this as a positive result – you got some value out of the experience – a piece of learning. It may have been expensive but you bought it so don't leave it in the shop.

All practical learning comes from action and experience – so you've learned something the hard way. Unfortunately, the hard way is often the best way.

I can assure you that my most expensive mistakes will NEVER be repeated, EVER.

2. Kiss It Goodbye
The failure is in the past. You cannot get to it and you cannot change it. Imagine it as a picture floating in the air in front of you. But it's moving away. It's getting smaller and smaller until...it's gone. Make sure you get the learning first, but then just let the image go.

Be determined to NOT let the failure colour your future negatively...that way you have made the failure bigger than it actually is. Don't empower the failure. Give it the kiss of death.

3. Recall a Past State
Getting back into a state you have been in previously that gave you success is a very useful technique.

Helpful states include feeling confident, feeling strong, feeling energised, feeling calm. There are many states.

When you want to get back into a particular state, recall a lucid past experience when you felt that state. Make sure you are really plugged into the experience, really "there", not just thinking about it.

Do this just before you want to regain the previously experienced state.

I often do this sitting in my car outside a potential client's premises. I imagine the last time a sales meeting went really well. And it really works. It's like having some kind of superpower.

4. Focus on What You Want
I think it was Mother Teresa who said something to the effect that she would never attend an anti-war rally, but she would attend a peace rally. The idea is that what you focus on increases. It is futile and counter-productive to focus on what you don't want. This is something that the protesters at St Paul's could do with realising.

Focusing on failure will bring failure. Focusing on success might bring success.

We are conditioned...
...to see failure as a terrible, dark horror.

Now, being lazy, shoddy, unfocused and undisciplined is a BAD THING, and you will kick yourself for that, and rightly so. But giving something a damn good shot and not getting the result you wanted is not a BAD THING.

So when you don't get the result you wanted, don't box it off and suppress the memory. Do one or more of these four things and you will be managing the setback rather than the setback managing you. This is resilience and resilience is one of the foundations of high performance.

In a Nutshell...

Handling setbacks and failures well is a key characteristic of high performers.

ARE YOU ASSERTIVE?

There are only four major behavioural types. And only one of these is any use.

The four types are...

Passive
Aggressive
Assertive
Passive-aggressive

The useful one is assertiveness, of course. This is because you stand not a snowball's chance in hell of developing self-confidence unless you are assertive.

Assertiveness is the ability to remain calm but firm under pressure.

Here are a few questions for you –

- Do you get upset very quickly when others question your views?

- Do you avoid difficult conversations?

- Do you say things you immediately regret?

- Do you agree with people when you really don't at all?

- Do you feel you have fragile self-esteem?

If you would answer "yes" to any of these questions on any kind of a regular basis, then that's indicative of your assertiveness skills being a bit rubbish really. This is not good for you and merits a wee bit of remedial action.

Whatever could the matter be?

Are you passive?
When you behave passively you tend to just let stuff happen. You usually don't speak up when you don't agree and even when you do speak up you are deferential and back down far too easily.

Being easy-going is one thing. Being passive is being a doormat.

Are you aggressive?
This is Mr Shouty. He's rude, makes threats and uses bullying. The occasionally aggressive person may be the passive person who has blown a fuse.

Are you assertive?
What characterises this saint-like behaviour? Well, usually it's –

- An ability to remain calm (relatively!) and

- An ability to stand your ground.

You are happy to listen to others as they do not intimidate you. You can be changed by a good argument but if not you will say so and hold firm. You may compromise and you will keep bashing away at the issue until a satisfactory outcome is reached.

Are you passive-aggressive?
I HATE this one. It's the silent treatment. The you've-got-to-guess-what's-wrong-with-me game. The use of silence or sulking or being deliberately obstructive are all signs of the passive-aggressive.

More subtle is the "poor me" routine. "I'm the only one who does anything around here..." and similar.

The tactic here is for the passive aggressive to get their own way by making you feel guilty. No chance.

So, how to be more assertive?

No 1…Right Think

Get your thinking right. Someone who works for you storm into your office, bitches about someone else in your team and asks you to go "and sort them out". You can be upset by your staff member confusing you with their Mum or you can say to yourself – "this person is clearly upset herself. I'll try to understand why this is and from there I can try to work out what, if anything, either of us should do."

No 2…Right Emotions

Get your emotions right. Having got your thinking right, the right emotions flow easily. Instead of feeling angry, or challenged, or burdened by your staffer, you feel OK. OK's fine in this situation. You are unruffled.

No 3…Right Behaviour

Get your behaviour right. Now that your emotions are correct, you will do the right things. You are assertive. You listen, you acknowledge your colleagues concerns and you focus on finding a solution with them. (Assuming this isn't a "no-solution-required" conversation, but that's another blog post).

No 4…Right Outcome

Get the right outcome. You agree a way forward with your team member. Relations are maintained and self-esteem is intact. (OK – this might not happen, but that doesn't mean assertiveness is a flawed strategy. Not everyone is rational all of the time and it takes two to tango).

Here's an exercise for you (no sulking)…

You know that difficult conversation you've been putting of for weeks (passive) because when you bring it up things degenerate into a shouting match (aggressive) and then the huffy/sulky thing (passive-aggressive)…? Well, get your assertive thinking cap on (as per the above example). This will lead to an emotionally neutral state instead of something worse. Then, sit down with the person and have the assertive conversation you need to have.

Dr Mark J Nugent

You may get an agreed solution. And even if you don't, that's OK. You tried. You will feel better because you have opened a door to self-development and in the long run you will get the desired result more often than not.

There's no gene for assertiveness. It's a mindset issue and it takes practice.

In a Nutshell...

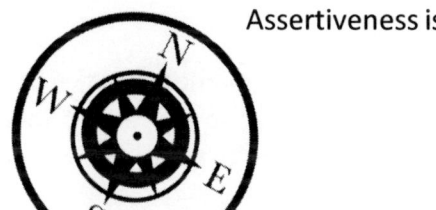
Assertiveness is the only route to self-confidence.

STOP THINKING ABOUT THAT

There shouldn't be lots of stuff on your mind. Having lots of stuff on your mind is like having someone tug your sleeve every three minutes.

The only thing that should be on your mind is the stuff you're doing right now – the stuff that's right in front of you. You should be "present", in the moment, focused on what you're doing. No sleeves being tugged.

The other stuff on your mind is stealing precious memory (think RAM) and is caused, I am afraid, by operator error. But as we've discussed before, the brain, although amazing, is tricky to use and there's no manual.

The operator error is one of poor housekeeping. The operator has failed to do the hoovering and the tidying up.

The reason stuff is on your mind is because you have not managed it, faced up to it, dealt with it, scheduled it. Whatever you should have done you haven't done it. The stuff on your mind is feeling neglected and is tugging your sleeve. Every three minutes. And you cannot hit it.

When your mind is like this there is a tendency to do what screams the loudest or is the easiest. That might be the right thing to do next, but probably isn't.

So you get a double hit – the sleeve tugging makes it impossible to do your best on whatever it is you're working on and whatever it is you're working on is probably not the right thing anyway because you only chose it because it was screaming or because it appeared easy. Oh dear.

Our mind should be left alone to focus on the current, present task without any RAM being consumed by the sleeve tuggers.

So, what to do?

Take all of the stuff that's on your mind and write it down on a piece of paper. For all the small stuff, diary an hour and just do it. Yes, I did just use diary as a verb. For the big stuff, decide if there's anything you want to and can do about it. If there isn't, just let it go. Kiss it goodbye, say sorry, accept it as part of the messiness of life – whatever you have to do to let it escape. And don't chase after it.

If there is something you want to and can do about it, turn the issue into a goal. A **SMART** goal. Decide if you have the time to make this goal one of your current goals. If not, put it on a list of stuff to come back to later and make sure you do come back later.

If you do wish to adopt it as a current goal, decide on the next thing to do and put that activity in your diary. When the appointed time comes, do the thing, decide what the next thing is and put that in your diary. Repeat to fade.

You will have to do this housekeeping exercise regularly, maybe once a week.

You will be amazed at how this frees up your mind, your RAM. You have made an intelligent decision about what to do and it is in process – the next step is in the diary. There is no more you can do. You are in control. You have self-managed. And you have freed up the greatest thing ever seen in the universe – your mind – to actually focus on the things you have decided merit focus. A great resource used wisely by a skilled operator. It's not a guarantee of success, but it's pretty close.

What would you like to stop thinking about today?

In a Nutshell...
If something's on your mind and bothering you, it's because you haven't dealt with it. So deal with it.

PRESENT AND CORRECT?

Or.....You might be in the room, but where exactly are you?

I have a predilection for being future-focused. I have a strong preference for having goals and milestones and plans and all that jazz. I am always looking forward, thinking about tomorrow, trying to create a future...

I used to find it quite hard to be present. To be here, now, in this moment. To take some time to smell the roses. To enjoy the journey as much as the destination. But it never bothered me until I started up my own business where the challenges are such that you really can disappear right up your own...future, if that is your focus and you're not very careful.

I also had this sort of nagging feeling that not being present is not quite right somehow. When dealing with people, not being present might be a wee bit disrespectful, maybe a bit lazy, maybe even a tad self-absorbed, dare I say!

I then read that one of the real focus areas for sports psychologists is to get their charges totally present. Now that makes sense to me – if you are just about to attempt some wonderful physical feat, you really need to be there, don't you. Not much point in thinking about next week's game while you're playing this week's game.

Now work and life is not sport. But presence is required in all realms. There is a need for us to look forward and plan, envision, think big thoughts and look after projects and all the rest of it, but getting good stuff to happen to you and avoiding bad stuff happening to you will depend on what you do now, in the present, and being present while you do it.

And stuff is often about people. People need you to be present. Not paying lip service to them. Not a million miles away.

And I actually have a slightly gnawing feeling that not being present is a wee bit like…not being alive. Hmmm. Time for action.

So, I started to think about how to become more present. This is what I found worked for me –

- Get physical – take a deep breath and see what's in front of you. Really see it. Tap your feet on the ground. Touch the table in front of you. Feel the temperature. Get aware of your surroundings.

- Get mental – say to yourself "I'm here! I'm here!"

- Get focused – one thing at a time – the thing in front of you.

- Get prepared – ask yourself what it is you want to remember about what you're doing.

- Get aligned – when talking to someone, make their objective your objective. This is a powerful one. When I was being taught how to give feedback on a certain psychometric tool, I used to try to run through it quickly. I was probably somewhere else, or trying to get there, i.e. not present. It was suggested to me I might like to make "helping the other person to understand her profile" my goal, which was, after all, why she was in front of me. Bingo – that worked! Told you I was self-absorbed.

All this effort to be more present actually works. I do have to practice though, but that's OK. I have to practice everything. That way I get better. I am more present more often. More alive. And that's no bad thing.

What are the benefits of being more present?

- Well, I think I have more fun, especially with my family. In fact with people in general.

- This in turn leads to better relationships.

- I feel more alive which is pretty good.

- Stress is reduced. A lot of stress comes from worrying about the past or the future. The here and now is less populated with stressors.

- I also think I actually get more done because I am more focused, clearer-headed and in the moment - you know the *actual* moment when I'm *actually* trying to *actually* do something. It's got to have an impact on productivity.

So, if you sometimes feel you're not really here, it's time to get present.

In a Nutshell...

If you want to do your best, you need to be present.

9/11, RESILIENCE AND YOU

It's the 11th September 2011 and I'm sitting in the foyer of the Marriott in San Jose.

It's 6.45 in the morning and the Starbucks is doing a brisk trade. I'm sitting here with a large Americano with an extra shot I really don't need. The sky is grey, as it has been every morning. The sun will soon rise high enough to burn the grey away, ushering in another beautiful Californian day.

I've been watching the 9/11 ceremony from New York with my fellow foyer dwellers and I am struck by the amazing resilience of this country. The amazing ability to recover, not just endure. To recover and thrive. Unbowed.

What does it take to be so resilient?

Identity
It takes identity. A positive view of who we think we are. The label we place on ourselves. This label can have many authors: parents, peers, authority figures and, most importantly, us. But I'm afraid the other authors are not always entirely helpful. But we don't have to let them write their bit on our label. We can and must define ourselves. This is the first part.

Interpretation of Events
Resilience requires us to interpret events in ways that help us, not hinder us. Information comes into our brains; we interpret it and decide what it means to us. This then defines our intentions and consequently the actions we take.

And there are two extremes to our interpretation –

a)   We set our goal; we didn't get the result we wanted; we are a failure; there's no point in trying again; we won't try again.

b)   We set our goal; we didn't get the result we wanted; we will try harder next time as we know we will get better; we want another chance; we go out and find that chance, now.

Same information. Different results. This is the second part.

Optimism

Resilience requires optimism. Optimism comes from sifting through our pasts for the good stuff and accepting the bad stuff as simply being "life". Optimism comes from looking at the here and now and asking ourselves "what do we have to be grateful for?" Optimism comes from looking at the future and being exciting about our possibilities.

And if there are any pessimists in our lives...we need to be careful here because they are toxic. There. I said it.

Self-Efficacy

Resilience requires self-efficacy. Basically self-efficacy is our belief that we can control an outcome or event. A lot of people lose their self-efficacy between the ages of 16 and 26 when they realise they aren't going to be a rock star etc. etc. Self-efficacy is a real differentiator. If we don't have self-efficacy...we're in real trouble.

These four factors are the foundation stones of our resilience.

Each of them is a practice. They are not absolute. They are mental constructs. We construct what we want –

- We can contribute to our identity along with others or we can claim it all to ourselves.

- We can interpret events in any way we want (really).

- We can be optimistic or pessimistic; glass half full or half empty.

- We can believe we have control or we can believe we have no control – whichever we believe will be our reality.

Our choices on these four factors are major contributors to our resilience.

I'm not going to score the USA on the four elements of resilience. The USA is self-evidently resilient because it chooses to be.

OK, so what about us humans, rather than nations?
We are getting closer to the core here. The nub. The heart of the matter.

When we wrap it all up – identity, interpretation, optimism, self-efficacy and resilience – we find that this defines what is currently understood by psychologists to be our psychology. Our psychology. Definition – the study of our mind and its functions.

So maybe we should look at ourselves and ask "what's our psychology?"

Well that's a big issue for a blog post, but let's start with IDENTITY.

Here's something to think about -
List the five most irritating "ingredients" that have been scrawled on your identity label. You may not think they are big issues, and they may not be. But if they happened years ago and they are still popping into your brain, they are still with you. And although they may not be doing you much harm it is unlikely they are doing you much good. And your identity is supposed to be for your good. So it's time for action.

Again, list the five most irritating "ingredients" that have been scrawled on your identity label. By your parents (even although they loved you), your peers (even although they were kidding) and the authority figures you met when you were young and sensitive.

Look at the list. Does it describe you? If not, let it go. We are our own architects. We design ourselves. The people that said this stuff about us, they meant no harm. And if they did, even more reason to let it go.

The sun's coming out. There's 350 million people here, and not one of them knows me...my identity is what I choose it to be. Now, where's the keys to the Aston.

In a Nutshell...
It's not about avoiding setbacks; it's about how you react to them.

WHEN IT'S GOOD TO EXTERNALISE

I'm forever banging on about "not externalising". And I'm usually right to do so. It usually isn't good to externalise – to blame events, other people or circumstances for your results. This is bad. It's a victim mindset and leads to even more bad results. Internalising is the thing to do – asking yourself what you can do to feel better/get a better result – whatever it is that's bugging you.

But there is one situation when externalising is precisely the approach to take. It's actually a different kind of externalisation. It's not about blaming something or someone else. In this case, by externalisation I mean simply yanking something out of your brain to work on it, rather than trying to do all the heavy lifting inside your head.

You see the problem is that we humans are surprisingly rubbish at working stuff out in our heads. Our thoughts and feelings bounce around like so many careering pinballs setting off flashing lights and buzzers in a blinding cacophony that seldom seems to yield an optimal solution.

So we need to get the issue out of our heads. We need to externalise.

There are two ways:

Firstly, write it down.
Whatever the problem may be. A number of years ago when I was still employed someone asked me if I'd like to be put forward for a job in another company. It was a senior position. I kicked it around in my head for days and days and couldn't get a clear view on what I thought. There were pros and cons. My gut feeling was to go for it, but I held back. There must have been a reason. After about a week, and after being chased, I wrote it issue down… "Should I go for this job?" and I then compiled a list of pros and cons. The pros column had one entry. I was shocked. One entry. The cons column had about eight

or ten. It was a no brainer. (Ha!) Maybe quite literally: I didn't need my brain to work out the answer. In fact, my brain was hindering me.

OK, so far so obvious.

But the point is that this writing-issues-down thing is also called keeping a journal. Not a diary. But a journal where issues are worked on, problems solved, decisions made. We are much better at solving problems when they are outside of us. When we have externalised them.

Secondly, we can externalise our issue by speaking about them.
Have you ever come up with the answer to something just by talking to someone about it – even if they don't actually say anything? In fact, it is better if you can choose someone who will not try to give you the answer, but instead will prompt and assist until you get there yourself. So avoid the "well this is what I'd do if I were you…"-types, (that's most men out of the running!)

This second approach is, of course, the basis of coaching. Sometimes I help my clients just by being there and gently and infrequently guiding the conversation. It took me a while to get used to that, initially being of the male disposition of I-must-be-the-omnipotent-oracle. As if.

So, if you find your mind invaded my persistent thoughts about an issue that never seem to reduce down to a simple solution, externalise the problem. Write it down or talk to a well-chosen listener.

Personally, I'd start with writing it down, in a journal. You will find, in time, that "journaling" becomes a natural activity that you quickly turn to whenever you sense one of those persistent and difficult issues is brewing in your brain. Keeping a journal clarifies thinking quickly and effectively. You can then simply look at the answer you have come up with and get on with doing what you need to do, instead of playing endless pinball with your thoughts and emotions.

As I've said many times before, the human brain is absolutely magical but it is not always easy to use and there is no user guide. So, maybe consider this post another page in your personal My Brain - User Guide, entitled "How to deal with issues that stubbornly don't resolve in my head – EXTERNALISE."

In a Nutshell...

Some problems are not easily solved in our heads. Getting them out on the table often gives the perspective needed to solve them.

EXCELLENCE

We are creatures of habit. Habit is powerful and is a great force for good....or bad. Success is measured by the extent to which we reach our goals. That, in turn is determined by what we do.......our behaviours. Behaviours are driven by our attitudes. And our attitudes are HABITS of thought. It's worth saying that again......our attitudes are HABITS of thought.

We can form habits for the good........set goals, do all the things we need to do to achieve our goals, develop internal motivation, determination, a winning attitude, and take MASSIVE ACTION.......

Or, we can form bad habits.......don't set goals or set poor ones, don't do what we need to do to be successful, or do too little, allow external forces to motivate us, give up too easily, settle for mediocrity and take only MODEST ACTION.

This is our choice. In time, each leads to radically different outcomes.

Psychologists have shown that most habits can be broken and replaced by new ones in only 21 days. Three weeks of discipline and then the habit takes care of itself. A good habit is no more difficult to maintain than a bad habit. Only 21 days to choose a better road to travel. And today is day 1......

In a Nutshell...
Our habits make us for good or bad.

THE FIRST 60 MINUTES REALLY MATTER

I've been playing around with a morning routine, or ritual, for a few weeks now.

Why?

Well, I know of some people who swear by their morning routine. So I thought I'd give it a go. Plus, I know from observing myself that when I've had some form of routine in the morning that kick-starts me and focuses me it can help to avoid the admittedly infrequent occasions when I don't really get started and I end up having one of those unproductive, frustrating days that drive me nuts.

So, a wee while ago I put together my first proper morning routine. It looks like this –

1. Get Up – good start.

Set the alarm and allow myself one press of the "snooze" button. When it goes off a second time I get up. That's 18 minutes snoozing.

2. Drink - loads.

Descend stairs and drink a large glass of water while the kettle boils. Make coffee.

3. Exercise – so early!

Do 30 minutes of stretching and weights whilst listening to Mahler in my 37th attempt to get into classical music.

4. Plan The Day – it's not the plan that matters, it's the planning (General MacArthur).

Most of what I need to do is already in the diary: client facing time; high-payoff activities. But I just make sure I am absolutely clear what else I must do before the working day is over.

Dr Mark J Nugent

5. Eat – full English!

You must be joking. I'm talking protein shake. I love eating but this is not part of the love. It is a system reboot. Just do it.

6. Get presentable – you may get run over.

Shower/dress etc.

That's it. Fifty to sixty minutes all in.

It covers the bases –

- Physical – exercise is great and eating is good.
- Mental – planning the day is good for the psyche.
- Emotional – the major emotional component is also the exercise. I cannot tell you how relieved I am after doing thirty reps of the trunk twist while lying on my back with my knees in the air, clutching a 6kg medicine ball between the aforementioned knees. I have dropped the ball once. That will not happen again. Plus, with the exercise I'm wired on endorphins (and Guatemalan coffee).

Keeping to the routine was a bit hard for the first two weeks. As always, I overdid it and tried to stick to it for 7 days/week. Now it's 5 days/week – the working days. I do get up earlier so that I can have it done by 8/830-ish.

I am aware that it takes about three weeks to establish a habit but once you have the habit things get easier. You make your habits and then your habits make you. (Many people claim to have coined this phrase but the first guy was my main man Aristotle).

So, has this been worthwhile?

A resounding "yes!" to that:

I think the key is the exercise. It stretches my muscles and kick-starts my system. And equally importantly, exercise also touches me emotionally – it just lifts me. It makes me happy. Like I said - endorphins. So the exercise is a big, big plus.

Eating is also good. I have never, ever felt hungry in the morning so the great temptation is to skip breakfast. But when I actually eat breakfast (especially a protein shake) it's like a massive switch inside me has been slammed into the ON position.

And finally, despite invariably having my day filled with high-payoff activities, it is good just to spend ten minutes really, really defining what tasks I must do today and I will not stop until they are done. Never start the day until you have finished the day on paper (as Jim Rohn said. Aristotle would have liked Jim).

I still resist the discipline of the morning ritual but I am beginning to love it and it has huge benefits.

If I persevere for another week or so my morning routine will become a habit that I will have made and then I can allow the habit to make me...

In a Nutshell...
What you do in the first hour of the day really matters. The return on this investment can be massive.

How To Do Anything

I have mentioned the power of routines. I'm going a bit deeper on this topic here.

Routines can help us to do things we don't really want to do. I'm talking about doing this thing you don't like every day (or so), until it becomes a routine. This works because routines become automatic. "I've always done it this way." Not so good if we're talking 3 hours of TV every night. A bit better if we're talking 20 minutes exercise before 7.30am.

It starts with willpower. The sheer will to begin to do something. Willpower is a great force but there are two things you need to be aware of. Firstly, willpower is in short supply. Don't confuse its immediate power with consistency. Willpower is soon depleted. It is difficult to use willpower in the long term to achieve anything. Secondly, using willpower, or indeed any power, is draining. There's less left in the tank.

This is where routines come in. Leverage willpower by establishing routines. Like my morning routine. A little power goes a long way because it kicks off a routine. The willpower required is tiny - it is the willpower required to get up as soon as the Blackberry alarm's first snooze is over. That's the willpower. Not much. And the leverage is the routine – the main benefit of which is that I exercise and actually eat some breakfast.

This is the efficient and effective use of willpower.

The 800-pound gorilla in the room is our old friend: fear. Fear – the enemy of will. Fear needs to be managed.

There's no time here for a treatise on fear but try this – when you feel fear, recognise it, accept it for what it is (some ancient obsolete brain function designed to protect you from something that wanted to eat you over by the swamp), wonder about the poor caveman or woman that needed that protection, and then do what it is you want to do anyway, after checking for sabre-toothed tigers.

So can you really use will power, routine and fear management to do anything you want? Well I think you can. And that's 90% of the battle, for me. I don't accept I cannot do something. Sometimes I have been shown to be wrong but that's not the point. It's the attitude that matters. Going back to golf, the sports psychologists say you should look at every putt with an overwhelming certainty that it will sink AND to not mind if you miss. This seems internally inconsistent but it is actually management of the fear of failure by understanding that failure is not personal, merely a result you didn't want.

So how do we put all this together –

1. Design the routine first. Maybe a morning routine. A high-payoff activity you hate doing, e.g. making 20 phone calls a day; speaking to a group. Whatever it is. Routine-ise it. What are you going to do? Where are you going to do it? When are you going to do it – time and frequency?

2. Then apply willpower. Use sparingly, as a catalyst, to begin the routine. Let's say you want to do your routine every working day. It will take about three weeks for your routine to become so engrained that you won't need to use any willpower at all after that. You have a new habit. We're 80% robot. We can use this to our advantage by setting up routines.

3. From the start, manage any fear you have. Recognise it, accept it, but remain unchanged by it.

Worth a try? What's the worst that can happen? Good luck.

In a Nutshell...

Willpower does not work alone. It is in short supply. But there's a solution.

THE SEVEN HABITS STILL RING TRUE

It's not often I re-read a book. In fact the only book I have re-read is Roald Dahl's **Danny the Champion of the World**. But I have just finished re-reading Stephen Covey's masterful **The 7 Habits of Highly Effective People**. The worst thing about this book is the title. It sounds like just another quick-fix, get-everything-you-want-in-5-minutes fantasy. But it isn't.

So here are the habits, neatly summarised -

No 1 Be Proactive
We are in charge of ourselves. We are responsible – ***response-able***. We can choose how to react to external stimuli, rather than being Pavlov's dog – salivating at the light.

Covey says that keeping to your commitments – to yourself and others – is the clearest manifestation of our proactivity. If we commit to do something – do it. If we don't want to commit to it – don't commit to it. Integrity to our commitments is the clearest manifestation of our proactivity.

No 2 Begin With The End In Mind
All things are created twice – first in our minds and then in reality. We need to get clear on what we want – then create it. It's goal setting, essentially.

Without clear goals we are adrift. I reckon roughly 80% of people have no clear goals. They're not bad people. They're just won't realise their potential.

No 3 Put First Things First
This is the high-payoff activities I bang on about endlessly. Not the crises, deadlines, interruptions and endless small stuff. We must learn to say "no" to everything that is not a high-payoff activity. Say "no" to others, and to ourselves. Do it pleasantly, smilingly, non-apologetically. But do it. Time actually IS our greatest asset.

No 4 Think Win-Win

In all relationships – business and personal. Life is not a zero-sum game. To win, others do not have to lose.

Do you have any win-lose relationships in your life? Turn them into win-win, or politely excuse yourself and go. Win-lose is bad for the other guy and bad for your soul. It's actually lose-lose.

No 5 Seek First To Understand

...then to be understood.

People want to be understood, but few people do the understanding. Why not be one of them? When I meet people for the first time I make sure the conversation is about them, not me. Shamefully, I started doing this because it was suggested to me that this would help them to like me, as people like those who are interested in them. Fortunately, I now find myself genuinely interested in understanding them first. I enjoy understanding them. I actually like it. They seem to too. Maybe I really am a coach.

No 6 Synergy

1 + 1 = 3. We work better when we work together. I'd rather be in two ventures, sharing the profits with another human being, than in one venture by myself. I'm pretty good. I've got the test results to prove it. But I'm not that good. I lose perspective pretty quickly by myself. I miss things. I don't see clearly. I am glad I am sufficiently self-aware to see this.

No 7 Sharpen the Saw

Take time to renew. You cannot work all the time. We need to rest, reflect, renew. So take some exercise, write a journal (a great idea), just play, or take time with someone you love. I'm rubbish at all of this. Someone said to me the other day they were leaving the office at 4pm to go home. I thought to myself – "what a luxury." It's not a luxury. It's a necessity.

I cannot do Covey's book justice in these few words. I suggest you read it, or re-read it and you, like Danny, can be champion of the world.

In a Nutshell...
There is no hidden magic to being effective. Effective people do these seven things. This book is a classic for a reason.

SHARPEN THE SAW

Stephen Covey recommends in his "The 7 Habits of Highly Effective People" that we "sharpen the saw".

He talks about a man spending all day struggling to fell trees with a blunt saw. When asked why he doesn't sharpen the saw, he says "I don't have time for that."

Sound familiar?

Covey advocates taking some time out to rethink what we do, to refresh and to exercise. And to come back sharper, stronger and more focused.

Well, I did it, properly for the first time ever. In 22 years of business.

What did I do in my four days of saw sharpening?

I reviewed my business performance in the last year. Fully and honestly. Where my business came from. How I won it. Whether the business I won played to my strengths. Were the customers really in my target market segment? Did they truly value what I did? Did the commissioning managers engage with me, or did they just want me to "sort that lot out"?

And the really fabulous customers...did I give them as much as I could have? Could I have loved them even more?

I then planned for the coming year. To go back to my values and to derive a strategy based on them. With planning better than ever before. And fewer, better, performance measures. With goals that are challenging but achievable. To decide what to do and, critically, to decide what not to do.

And I exercised. Almost every day (since mid-December). In the fresh air, in the snow, in the rain. Fabulously head-clearing.

Was all this worthwhile? A resounding "yes" to that.

So, what did I get out of this outrageously indulgent activity over the last week?

1. I know what worked for me last year, and what didn't. And I have resolved to do more of what worked and, of course, to stop doing what didn't work. And this involves key relationship management...I have many more business relationships than those that are truly key.

2. I know some of my customers are great for my business and some less so. This is a perennial issue in smaller organisations (and big ones, but often more debilitating in the former). But it's my fault, and I will fix it. Better definition of target market segment is the answer, coupled with a default "no" to those outside it, rather than a default "yes". To those inside it – give them ever more love and attention.

3. I have an excellent plan for this year to significantly grow my business and I feel that it is achievable. This will require some real changes. Of course it will. Scary? A bit. But it is wildly motivational. Wildly!

4. I have really experimented last year with delegating which for me means outsourcing – if I can get someone to do all the stuff that is not immediately and directly linked to me delivering my plan, then get them to do it. This has been a success in the past year and I shall continue to do it.

5. After four days with only a pad, a pen and some books, and little or no activity with anything involving a screen, no matter how sexy (the screen, that is), I am astonished, anew, at the power of spending uninterrupted time on the important stuff. And doing this stuff first, rather than "clearing the decks" of the trivia, which is the same as prioritising the small stuff over the big stuff. Now that really is bizarre.

6. The default position of just getting on with things and having the same year as last year is a powerful force that most succumb to and I certainly have many times. This force is with me, but will be defeated!

7. I do too much. Have been doing this for years. I get involved in things because they might make money or are interesting or new. But they do not accord with my values. Which means I don't follow through effectively, they turn into chores and I end up having to back out...

Hence my strategy for this year is derived from my values and a zero-tolerance approach to all other business activity.

8. Waiting another year (or, shamefully, much longer...) to sharpen again the saw is not an option.

I'll wait 13 weeks. Once a quarter to sharpen the saw...it's not a luxury, it's a necessity. And it's already in the diary.

9. Keeping a journal is a great idea. Not a diary. But a journal of regular reflections on personal performance and a place to assess new directions and opportunities...on an on-going basis to fill the gaps between dedicated saw-sharpening time.

10. I've always been a "learner" – educating myself, for fun and profit. But sometimes learning goes on the back burner. And "on-the-job" learning is a poor surrogate for the real thing. No more – I have now formalised learning into a high-payoff activity, to take pride-of-place in my diary alongside the other high-payoff activities.

So...I got all of this out of four days (less than 2% of my working year). Possibly the greatest investment with the highest return I will make this year, I suspect.

In a Nutshell...

You cannot run a machine 24/7 without maintenance. People are the same.

I Love Failure and You Should Too

I'm so rubbish at golf. Came 94th out of 96 last Saturday. Aarrgghh! (I take some solace from the fact that there were twelve bad boys and girls who failed to return their scorecard, presumably because if it isn't recorded it never happened, right?)

I am not scared of failure. I have got used to it. As the American golfer Tom Watson famously said – "if you want to double your rate of success, double your rate of failure." I must be getting pretty close to a major breakthrough as I have upped my failure rate significantly.

So, how do you double your rate of failure?

Well, there are two forms of failure –

Failure through action...

And...

Failure through inaction.

Hmmm.

Let's take the first one first:

Failure through Action
This is absolutely forgivable. We do stuff. We review what happens. We make changes because we didn't quite get what we wanted. Simple. What happens if someone – your boss, loving spouse, yourself – gives you a kick up the backside because you didn't get the exact results you forecast? Well you could be forgiven for avoiding getting things wrong again by swerving all challenging stuff as it comes to you. This is bad.

Or you could just jab a pointy stick in your tormentor's eye and say "there is no failure, just results I didn't want, you numbskull."

The more stuff you do the more you find out what works and what doesn't. And provided the mistakes are stopped early, the learning can be extracted from them at low cost. This works in marketing. It works in most fields. Fail quickly and cheaply and you quickly build a huge reserve of knowledge on what **does** work. There is no success without failure. But you still need to manage risk of course. No failure should be bigger than it has to be. We should not be fearful of failure, we should be fearful of the absence of failure because that's symptomatic of inaction which takes me nicely to ...

Failure through Inaction
This is insidious as it is often invisible. Fear of failure tends to be more focused on action: doing things and failing, rather than inaction...not doing things and failing.

Now clearly if you are observably not doing something you should be doing you will get pulled up for it. And rightly so. Where failure through inaction is at its most dangerous is when the inaction is about failure to behave in a certain way. I'm using "behave" in its neutral form – how we conduct ourselves. Nothing to do with "bad" or "good" behaviour.

I'm talking about staying inside your comfort zones: that mental straight jacket that we all have. And not taking managed risks. Not having the difficult conversations. Not reflecting and making changes. Becoming stuck in our ways. Keeping the song inside us.

Looking inside ourselves and taking the right actions may well be the making of us and they are very unlikely to break us. It really is an asymmetric bet – the upside is bigger than the downside. If you place a small number of bets where the upside is bigger than the downside you make a bob or two. If you place hundreds of these bets, you get rich...

Of course there are risks but when you are considering doing something a wee bit "out there" ask yourself – what's the worst that can happen? Could I get back to the pre-action reality or am I irredeemably lost at sea? How can I de-risk this?

And here's a great question – "What's the risk in doing nothing?" People often think doing nothing has no risk. This is seldom true.

So here's my challenge to you for this short week. It's in two parts –

1. Stop doing something that you thought would give you a benefit but simply isn't. I'm talking about ACTIONS that may be difficult to stop but are FAILING and therefore should be stopped.

2. Start doing something that may take you forward. Trial it and see what happens. I'm talking about ACTIONS that may seem difficult but might help you SUCCEED. Manage the risks. Do it for a short while and review. Then make changes if necessary, and keep going.

There is no failure. It's just feedback. And we need feedback don't we?

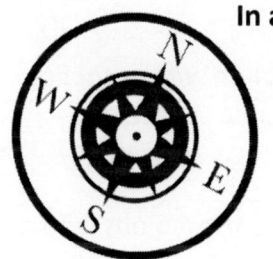

In a Nutshell...

There is no failure. Just results. Beware of seemingly avoiding failure by inaction. This is a trap.

FREE WILL

Of all the beasts on the earth only we humans have free will.

No bruises please...
In this life, we can strive, or hide. For some, life is about getting to the end with the fewest bruises (and the maximum number of regrets I suspect).

Good plan? Not for me.

I just can't help it...
You may think that you can't afford the time to strive for more....there's too much stuff to get out of the way, piling up, endless. But your time is yours. You have free will.

Most of what you do if you do it unthinkingly is due to conditioning. Conditioning gives you an automatic response mechanism to most situations. This is great because you don't have the time to work out how to talk to a person you've never met; how to dress for a certain occasion; how to cross the road; which part of the knife to grasp.

Autopilot...
But conditioning is a kind of autopilot. The problem with autopilot is that it flies you straight and level at an "acceptable" speed.

The Eagle Has Landed
On July 20th 1969, the Eagle landed on the moon. It did not land on autopilot.

Conditioning is a blessing and a curse. Use this autopilot for the basics in life. But for the good things in life you need to be flying on manual.

In a Nutshell...

We have free will but we often don't use it.

LIMITING BELIEFS

"Every man takes the limits of his own field of vision for the limits of the world." – Arthur Schopenhauer

Oh what a mess...
Some time ago, the then British Home Secretary Alan Johnson is responsible for the government's drug policy. He used the Advisory Council on the Misuse of Drugs (ACMD) to advise him.

High class...
The government has recently returned cannabis to Class B, reversing its previous demotion to class C. (Incidentally, the classification relates to harm caused: C = bad; B = worse; A = don't be stupid).

The chairman of the ACMD, Professor David Nutt, has accused ministers of devaluing and distorting evidence and said drugs classification was being politicised. He believes cannabis should have remained at Class C.

Got any horse?
Now, Professor Nutt, through his independent publicity unit, has recently pronounced that taking ecstasy (Class A, alongside heroin), is no more dangerous than riding a horse. There have been some other lurid comparisons as well. Mr Johnson retorted that few of his drug-addled Hull constituents had cause to worry about falling off a horse and promptly sacked Prof Nutt. His colleagues are now threatening to resign.

Some already have.

What a mess.

So who's right?

No one.

Each is wrong, independent of the other. But the scientists are more wrong so I'll concentrate on them.

Limiting beliefs...
The scientists and their supporters believe that they are right, and therefore it is right for their rightness to be fully enshrined in government policy, because after all policy is simply their rightness turned into an action plan. And if this does not happen, their rightness allows them to go public with lurid comparisons with scant regard for the impact they may have on all concerned.

This is called a limiting belief because it limits the scientists' ability to do their job – to influence government.

That's a classic...
It's actually a classic limiting belief that's been around forever, and afflicts scientists. The scientists' with this limitation believe that absolute truth is all there is. This is noble, but only in the lab and the pages of peer-reviewed journals. In the messy real world there is more to think about. The government is not obliged to simply turn scientific advice into policy. In this case, where the issue of harm arises, there is no effective truth to promote anyway, because few consumers actually think they are going to come to any harm. But Alan Johnson is not the first politician to ignored scientific advice.

Red alert...
In the cold war, John von Neumann was a scientific advisor to President Eisenhower. He developed game theory to calculate how each side in a two-player game can minimise their losses. It seemed clear that the Russian spy network had obtained many of the details of the US atom bomb design and it was only a matter of time before the Soviet Union became a nuclear power to rival the US. Von Neumann therefore recommended to Eisenhower that the U.S. launch a nuclear strike at the Russians, as now was their window of opportunity. The huge advantage the US had in possessing the atomic bomb would soon be lost. Game theory says that the US should have pressed home their advantage when they had the chance in order to

avoid a far worse war later. Von Neumann was right, within the limited scope of his analysis.

Clearly, Eisenhower, who had been around a bit, ignored him. So what are your limiting beliefs? If you have any recurring problems in your life, look under the surface. There might be a limiting belief lurking there.

In a Nutshell…
Limiting beliefs limit us, as their name implies. This is usually because we hold the "belief" to be almost a "truth", but this is wrong.

ATTITUDE

Your attitude is your choice
It might be a choice you made some time ago, some years ago. But it is a choice none the less. Your environment played a big part, the people you knew, your upbringing. But it's still a choice.

And it's critical...
...because it defines how you behave. And your behaviour defines your results. And your results deliver your goals. Attitude is that critical.

I don't see many...
...cynical, negative, inward-focused success stories walking around. Do You? Well maybe Mr Burns in the Simpsons.

Some people make a habit out of a bad attitude. Make a career out of it. It appears that the bulk of journalists, although smart, have chosen to adopt an attitude of great cynicism where everything is either black or white, and usually black.

I don't read...

...newspapers anymore. But I am interested, of course. So I read The Economist because it seeks to understand and inform and has a fundamental belief that humans can and will sort things out. Faith in humanity – what a great attitude.

Women – Know Your Limits!
Remember the Harry Enfield sketch – "Women – Know Your Limits!" We laugh, but most people do know their limits. Or what they think are their limits. Some people have a firmer grip on what they cannot do than what they can. And the more they know their limits the lower they seem to be. These are barriers. The ones in your heads of course are the real ones.

If you think...

...you'll lose, you're right. If you think you'll win, you're right.

Destroy all BMWs...

You should manage your attitude. You should use it positively, hold it to account, give it standards to aspire to and hit it with a stick when it lets you down. Do a daily attitude health check. Be on the watch for all bad thinking; placing blame on external factors; all thinking that does not serve your purpose.

Have no time for all **B**itchers, **M**oaners and **W**hiners. Don't let these people colour your attitude and hold you back. Demand more of your own attitude. Your attitude is a choice. Choose a good one.

In a Nutshell...

Attitude is a choice and plays a huge role in your results.

VALUES

What do you really value?

You probably sort of know, a bit. But have you really thought about it, and written your values down. And made sure that what you're trying to do in your life and work accords with your values. Because if it doesn't, you're running at a brick wall.

In tune, or out of tune...

It's difficult to be a happy nurse if you don't value service and kindness. I have had reason to visit a hospital on a good few occasions over the last few years. It was clear to me that the majority of the nursing staff took no joy from service or kindness. I know not why, but they were miserable, and it showed, and coloured the days of those they were supposed to be caring for, and most of them weren't going home.

But then I see a nurse who has made a heroic effort to attend the funeral of her late patient. She had travelled across a city to be there, finishing her journey with a sprint up the crematorium driveway. And she was smiling.

Values in tune with work = happiness. Values in discord with work = misery (and not just for you).

Useless values...

I look at bankers (the financially innovative ones, not the bulk of them)...what are their values? Well it's probably money and winning. They have a role to play. Investment banking allocates capital efficiently throughout our economy and that's essential. As a service. A service to our economy. But when the service runs the risk of destroying the served, as the banks almost did recently, their anti-social values need to be curbed by legislation and regulation.

I'll put you over my knee...

Meanwhile the government, who value being seen to do something...anything...try to avert a future crisis by curbing the salary and bonuses of the top guys. That's a bit like trying to bring up your kids by limiting the number of sweets they get. Necessary but insufficient.

All change...

Values do change over time. And people can find that their job and environment no longer accord with their changing and evolving values. Their buttons are no longer being pressed. And we need our buttons to be pressed. That's what they're for.

So what to do?

Simple: go to **www.HowToCoachYourself.net**, read the document and reflect on your observations. Make sure you have the right values, both for yourself and for the rest of us. Then act and become like the nurse who did a great thing, who felt compelled to do it, and couldn't stop smiling.

In a Nutshell...

What you do must reflect your values if you want to be happy.

FAILURE

"F" for Fail....

People experience failure. For some it is a short step to "I have failed." Then just another short step to "I am a failure." Once that mindset is established you are in big trouble.

I reach for my dictionary:

Failure – an event that did not produce the desired outcome.

What? Surely some mistake! There's nothing in this definition about you being a worthless failure who shouldn't waste your time striving for anything.

The problem is......

.....we judge ourselves. And this is a killer of self-confidence. *A killer.*

So the only really bad thing about failure is when you personalise it and turn it into a defining character trait of yourself or those around you. This is your choice. Choose to NOT do it. Give yourself and those around you a break. Where would we be if everyone was paralysed by fear of failure? Would things be better? There wouldn't be a light bulb in your cave.

Are you experienced?

Failure is an outcome you didn't want. Nothing more. It's not a character trait. It's not in your DNA. It's about events and outcomes.

As always, the difference between people is how they react to events. And there's really only two choices – give up or try again. Look up at the light bulb burning brightly above you, or its tubular offspring. Thank goodness Edison understood how unimportant failure is.

In a Nutshell...
Failure is simply a result you didn't want.

BEING AWARE

My Mother tells me time continues to speed up as you get older. Ug! It's already going past at 600mph. So fast that it's difficult to keep the really important stuff at the front of the mind. So easy to switch off the neck-top computer, do what we have always done and miss the chances to improve on last year, no matter how good last year was.

Well that would be a shame so here's my Top 10 list of self-management essentials to ensure you use the free will you most certainly have, but can so easily neglect.

Let's start at number 1...

Values
Straight in at number one, since about 5,000 B.C....values. What do you believe in? What matters to you? Values drive all effective action. Get this right. It's the foundation.

Purpose
Number 2...the angelic offspring of values....purpose. The essence of leadership – whether of oneself or of others. No purpose...no point. Start with values and from them...derive your purpose. Paying the mortgage is not a purpose. You were put on the earth for a wee bit more than that.

Plan
Number 3...values and purpose...now get a plan. You are part of a plan, whether you like it or not. The only question is who writes the plan. It's either you or someone else. If you don't wish to be the author there are many who will take your place, but they won't write the plan with you in the starring role.

Goals
Number 4...goals. You have a purpose...very good. Time to get a bit more real. A bit more tangible. So, how will I achieve my purpose? Goals. Goals. Goals. Think of goals as small steps on the route to achieving your ultimate purpose.

If you don't have goals get some help. I really mean it. When a coach/manager/mentor says to you to set goals, it's like your doctor saying "stop smoking." It's not fashion. It's not the latest thing. Just do it.

Action

Number 5...take massive action. Data collection is over. Thinking time is over. Define and focus on your high-payoff activities (the things that if you do NOT do, you will fail to achieve your goals). Work on your time management and personal productivity until you feel like you are in charge of yourself. Then you probably are. Develop a steely, cold, single-minded determination to do what you need to do to deliver your goals and ultimately your purpose. Consider throwing away your TV. Then throw it away.

Measure

Number 6...measure. If it matters to you, measure it. No measurement...no feedback. No feedback...no catalyst for improvement. You've got to get very lucky very early to be successful without measuring what's important. So, do you feel lucky? Well, do ya?

Fear

Number 7...fear. If you have a high-payoff activity that you do not do as much as you should, deal with the fear that stops you doing it. The mistake you're probably making is attributing more pain to doing the thing than not doing it. This is easy to do because the pain of doing the thing is now, palpable and tangible. Whereas the pain of not doing it is some time off and seems less urgent. Reattribute the pain to inaction, not action. In other words, focus on the pain of regret, not the pain of discipline, as the great, late Jim Rohn said. This works.

Educate

Number 8...educate yourself. Never stop. Deepen and widen what you know and how you use it. This is better than TV. You have the time.

Humans
Number 9...partner with others. We work better in teams. Get into one. Either a mentoring group, a mastermind group or a business partnership. Something involving others. We are social and work better in teams. But beware...here be dragons. Unless those you choose to work with are in the same place as you, mentally, and share similar ambitions, they will be very bad for you, despite not being bad people.

Stop running
Number 10...take time out. This life is a marathon, not a sprint. Smell the roses.

That's it. Why not focus on one of these areas right now...today. No matter how good the past has been, the future can be better. Good luck.

In a Nutshell...
We have free will. This is how to use it.

Motivation

Motivation....that which gives purpose.

Here we are again, another Monday for most of us. What will give us purpose today?

Well, there are three kinds of motivation:

Firstly there's **FEAR** motivation. Do this or I'll hit you with a stick/fire you. Does this motivate, give purpose? It can, for a while. It can be good to have a "burning platform" when affecting change in a business. But **FEAR** motivation is external to us; it is imposed upon us from outside. And it is temporary. People will find a way to shield themselves from the FEAR. Or get their own stick.

Secondly, there's **INCENTIVE.....**do this and I'll give you a large pile of money, carrot etc. Does this give purpose? It can do. But again, it's external and temporary. When the donkey's had a carrot it may not want another for some time. Or it may not do anything at all before the carrot is given - the incentive has become custom and practice. The drug no longer works.

Thirdly, there's **ATTITUDE** motivation. We find purpose and a reason to do what we need to do because we are crystal clear on our own personal, worthwhile goals. We have really understood what we want and where we are going and what we need to do to get there. We are in charge. We have our own map. Our **ATTITUDE** drives us. This is internal. This is permanent. It does not ebb and flow. It serves us well.

In a Nutshell...
The only true motivation comes from within us.

HOW TO STAY POSITIVE

Martin Seligman became President of the American Psychological Association in 1996. He made a bit of an impact straight away by telling his fellow psychologists that through their focus on illness they were missing an important point.

He suggested that if they focused on what was right with people and learn how to help people to stay that way, many psychological issues would either never occur or would disappear – prevention being better than cure.

It's amazing how many professions get this wrong – if you're 7 years old and a great creative writer, but cannot tell the time, your teacher may focus on the fact that you cannot tell the time, as if it is likely you will grow into an adult who cannot tell the time.

Almost all managers focus on the poor performers and not the star performers. They assume the high performers have little more to give. But surely it will be more rewarding to focus on those who are talented right out the box, rather than trying to drag those who are below average up to the average?

Some industries do get it right – top flight sports teams get it right. They do not focus on trying to raise the game of those who are below average. They let them go and they focus on the best – helping them to raise their game. This is leadership.

Jo Owen touches on this area in the recently published 2nd edition to his book *How To Lead*.

He interviewed 700 leaders and came up with the rather obvious conclusion that successful leaders are more positive that the rest. Now to me, "positive" is a state of mind that drives "positive" actions. This is not to be confused with wild optimism.

Owen suggests 7 areas where you can assess how positive you are -

1. Focus on strengths, not weaknesses
You cannot succeed by dealing with your weaknesses. Successful leaders focus on their own strengths and find others who have as strengths the leader's weaknesses.

2. Manage your feelings
Emotional intelligence. If you are upset or angry – understand that that is about your beliefs. No one has *made* you angry. Chose how to **be. Be** engaged. **Be** positive.

3. Visualise
Visualise success. Focus on the goal and how to get there. Can you articulate in simple words where you're going? Clarity of purpose. And ambition. But don't be scared...it is better to aim for 100 and hit 80 than aim for 40 because that's what you normally get, and then actually hit 40. Only you will know if your goal is really challenging, and if it is, and you miss by a bit, that's OK. The real problem is those who aim for 40, or, even worse, those who do not aim at all.

4. Do something worthwhile – which may or may not be in work.

If you are not doing something worthwhile, where you feel real purpose, you will struggle to remain positive. Leadership is not for everyone, and that's OK. But maybe you are a leader – just not where you are right now.

5. Move to action
Do not conduct a post-mortem on the past. It's gone. Do not have a victim mentality – don't blame others for your past misfortunes.

6. Wear the mask of leadership
No matter how you feel and sometimes you will feel like a bag of nails...no one wants to know, not really. Sorry about that. When they ask you how you are, they want you to say "great".

7. Take control
Even with your back against the wall you will have something you can do; something within your sphere of control; a lever you can pull. Do

not worry about the things you cannot control. Stay focused on what you can do. And do it.

This is all obvious stuff.

If you find yourself getting any of this wrong today, pull yourself up.

Why?

Well think of the alternative - ignore your strengths and try to eliminate your weaknesses; be at the mercy of your emotions; have no idea what success looks like; spend the prime of your life on stuff you don't find worthwhile; dwell on the past; moan; focus on what you cannot do and don't do it.

Yuk!

In a Nutshell...
You are wholly responsible for your state of mind.

OTHER GOOD MINDSET STUFF

How to Coach Yourself

Self-Confidence

Integrity

Self-Discipline

Procrastination - Part 1 - Causes of

Procrastination - Part II - Solution to

What's Your Big Skill? – 3 Tests

Do You Make Good Decisions?

What Drives Your Decisions – Pain or Gain?

Self-Confidence Revisited

Conditioning

Lizard Brain vs iBrain

Think You're Proactive? - take my test

Getting Some Help

 My Observations of Successful People

How Biased Are You?

Moral Hazard

Do You Focus on Strengths or Weaknesses?

What I Learned In 2009

What I Learned In 2010

What I Learned in 2011

How To Coach Yourself

I hate to admit this but a month or so ago I got myself a bit log-jammed. I mean I couldn't decide what I should be doing in my work. I don't mean I had a bad afternoon. Or an unfocused day.

This lasted for days. More days than I care to admit to. Quite frightening really.

During which time I messed around. I shuffled some papers. I did all the easy stuff.

I had three big objectives yet I couldn't knuckle down to any of them. So I did nothing (of importance). I am quite shocked at this because I should, and do, know better. But the logjam happened none the less. Like a football player losing form. I guess it can happen to the best of us.

"Physician, heal thyself" I can hear you all bellow.

Fair comment. So I did. And this is how I did it:

I coached myself. Well I'm supposed to be a coach so I coached myself.

I took myself through a classic coaching process coupled with some extra bits that work and some stuff from goal-setting best practice.

What was important was I gave myself the time to go through the entire process. It was like a system reboot. It wiped clean my confused and addled brain. I was like new.

If you're feeling a bit log-jammed, frustrated and feeling as if you're not really focusing on the most important stuff, have a look at the document. But you'll need at least 30 minutes, maybe a bit longer. But it could well be the best thing to do right now.

It really worked for me. The process got me to focus on priority number one (funnily enough, not the one I thought it was), and define and take the first step. And a lot more.

So I've now got a major goal achieved and I'm just about to start on the next one. The logs are all flowing down the river again.

Coaching – I love it.

You can get a copy of How To Coach Yourself here –
www.HowToCoachYourself.net

In a Nutshell...
A well-structured series of questions is often all you need to see clearly. Then it's all down to action.

Self-Confidence

Lack of self-confidence is a perennial problem. I am asked about it all the time.

You're on....GO!

I am reminded of a UK television advert that was shown a number of years ago. I think the sponsor was a sportswear brand, but as usual I cannot remember who. The camera is seeing what you see. You're looking down at your feet. You're wearing what appear to be football boots. You are standing on grass and there's a white line just in front of you. You look up and a well-known premiership manager is yelling in your face but the sound is distorted and you cannot make out what he says.

The floodlights are blinding...

You look out onto the field and three or four players are looking back at you, eagerly. They are all recognisable to anyone with a passing interest in English football. One of them is Wayne Rooney. They need you on, and now. You see the referee and he beckons you on. The well-known manager gives you a final piece of garbled advice and you sense you've just been pushed onto the pitch. The action starts and all around you is a blur of movement and shouting.

Do you feel confident?

Yes? – Good for you....you must be a professional football players or delusional. If, like me, you probably don't feel confident because you are not competent. To feel confident without competence is delusion.

What to do?

So how to become confident? Get competent, and to get competent you need to gain the skills you know you don't have, to move from conscious incompetence to conscious competence. Identify these shortcomings, and take action. Practise, read books, speak to those who have the skills, get educated...whatever it takes. As usual with me there's no gimmicks, no short cuts, no five-step plan. If you're really smart you will identify where you are unconsciously incompetent (you don't know what you don't know) and get competent at this too. You'll need help with that.

Other factors help in the road to self-confidence....
- know your beliefs and get rid of the ones that don't help you
- don't be dependent upon anyone or anything
- don't compare yourself to anyone
- don't compete with people (as Tiger Woods says "it's between me and the course, not the other players")
- understand you cannot give up anything you find desirable
- give up guilt
- set goals

And as always....
Take massive action. Do it now. Your actions will generate accomplishments, from which will flow your self-confidence. No gimmicks, no five-step plan. Just something that works...

In a Nutshell...
Confidence requires competence. Don't wait for confidence to appear. Generate it.

INTEGRITY

Being pregnant...

Integrity is a bit like being pregnant...you either have integrity or you don't. You either are principled, honest, scrupulous, faithful, consistent and trustworthy....or you're not.

I think there are a lot of people around who feel they have integrity but they'd be shocked at what others thought of them.

The person who over-claims on their expenses, has swine flu during the test match, lies to the taxman, parks in the disabled space.

Some tests...
Integrity is what you do when no-one's looking. It's the six o'clock news test – how would you feel if everything you said and did during the day was broadcast on the 6 o'clock News?

Mummy what did you do today?

It might be legal to help a company walk away from £80,000 of debt (as someone bragged to me the other day) but does it show integrity?

You are the law!

Another great test of integrity, and forgive me because I read it just the other day and cannot remember to whom I should offer credit...is to imagine everything you did became the law and everyone else had to comply...

Parking in the disabled spaces – everyone?

Insurance claim for a "stolen" camera whilst on holiday? – everyone?

Having swine flu during the test match – everyone?

Don't be so priggish...

Dr Mark J Nugent

Some of this stuff is trivial, some not. And pragmatic people skim over the small stuff saying it doesn't matter. But it does matter. It matters a lot.

When some very, very smart people working for a small energy company created a better business model in the gas market in the US it was profitable and sustainable and all was well. But some small "lapses" in their integrity became the norm and the small cracks became big cracks and soon the game was up, Enron was bust. The share price was near zero...everyone was out of a job and their pensions, which were invested solely in Enron stock...were valueless.

As day follows night...

Integrity is central to leadership, and the first person to lead is ourselves...to thine own self be true.

In a Nutshell...
You either have integrity or you don't. It's not a hat you wear when it suits.

SELF-DISCIPLINE

Self-discipline is what turns goals into achievement through the magic of action – the right ones at the right times. Not just the actions you like, but all of them.

We are not robots...
Sorry that's actually wrong. Perhaps a more accurate statement would be we have the potential to be more than robots. We are robots, for the majority of the time. But that's OK – we need most of what we do to be on autopilot. Otherwise, there's simply too much to think about. As robots, we move towards pleasure and away from pain; satisfying our desires, most of which are healthy and keep us alive and reproducing.

Higher ground...
However, it's a higher level function to reflect; to use our external eye, our self-awareness. Where we can see ourselves from somewhere other than the place where we live, just behind our eyes. To use this ability to gain insight and change what we do. To be better.

Self-discipline is not...
...doing what you like and calling it work (although it may be)
...pleasing yourself because it's pleasing to do so
...avoiding discomfort...easy

Self-discipline is...
...doing the important things first
...doing all the important things, not just the ones you like
...being your own leader
...ultimately your victory over the robot within you

So here's a test...
What's the most important thing you should be doing that...
a) is an ongoing activity, not a one-off?
b) will take your job/life/relationships (whatever) to a higher level?

Dr Mark J Nugent

And,

c) you are not comfortable doing?

I'm not talking trivial stuff here. Something that will really take you forward. Take some time to think.

What have you discovered..?

If you have no answer to this question you may be either a) a self-actualising mega-being or b) a robot that is following your programming by avoiding the pain of self-reflection.

If you have an answer to the test question, and if you are doing this activity, then you are self-disciplined.

If you're not doing this activity, then I'd say, at this point, you are not exhibiting self-discipline. (That is not to say you are not capable of it, or have not exhibited it in the past).

Take control...

For those of you currently exhibiting self-discipline, you are probably aware that in time, the third criteria, the one about not being comfortable doing it, will become less of an issue. This is good. In time, you will develop the habit of doing this activity and you will find that you have transported this critical activity from outside your sphere of control (don't like it and don't do it) to inside your sphere of control (like it, or perhaps manage your dislike, and do it).

Well done.

Then you have to move on...ask yourself the test question again, and act accordingly.

Repeat to fade

This is on-going self-discipline. It is a series of battles in a war against being a robot: a war to be human.

What to do

Take your answer to the test question, which defines this important activity that you don't like. Do the activity. Don't find the time to do it. Schedule the time to do it. And then do it. And again, and again.

Search and destroy...
Discomfort around the stuff that matters is not to be avoided; it is to be identified, challenged and overcome.
And the more of these battles you win, the more human you are.
It is simple, but not easy...
But like most things; with repeated action, they don't get harder; they get easier.

In a Nutshell...
Self-discipline makes us more human.

PROCRASTINATION - PART 1 - CAUSES OF

I'll just...

I'll just make sure this email's gone, first...I'll just make a quick coffee, first...I'll just return that phone call to my friend/Mum/new girl in accounts with the swimming pool-blue eyes...I'll just have another fag, first...Oh! Is that the time? See you tomorrow.

Procrastination, the curse of the nation...

Why do we do it? Or, more accurately, why do we not do it? Why do we procrastinate? Maybe you don't, in which case I imagine you are so successful that one of your PA's is reading this for you, and is now reaching for the delete button because he/she knows this is not relevant for you.

I'm busy! I can't be a procrastinator...

Busy doing what? Running around doing exactly what you want, when you want, in the way you want...I've seen pretend busy done at expert level in every organisation I've ever worked in.

I'm as successful as I want to be...

I'm happy...I'm not ambitious....really? Good for you. For some, yes. For most, I don't believe you. It's more like simply accepting your lot. Coming to terms with your situation. Things are "OK". Your life is..."OK". This is called complacency.

Fear...

... of failure, of success. Whatever you can think of...someone's fearful of it. Or more accurately, has failed to manage this emotion effectively.

I really don't feel like it...

Oh diddums. I was listening to Radio 4's Woman's Hour the other day, as you do, and there were some ideologically pure feminists on...you know the type of person – educated but stupid. Who needs to think when they've got an ideology? Basically their argument was that you should never, ever, under any circumstances have sex with your partner if you are less than 100% keen to do so at that precise moment. Girls!!! Get a grip. Do it until you feel like it....don't wait to feel like it.

In a Nutshell...

Procrastination is natural. It is caused by fear and/or discomfort. If you procrastinate about something unimportant, that's OK. If you procrastinate about something important, like a High-Payoff Activity, you are in trouble.

PROCRASTINATION - PART II - SOLUTION TO

Blowing bubbles...
This advice on how to overcome procrastination is for those with "normal" levels of it. If you really never start anything ever, go and see a doctor, unless you are a goldfish for whom this is normal.

Ok - so what to do?
Set goals and achieve them. That's it. Dead simple.

Any idiot...
...can write a goal. It's the achievement that's a bit tougher. So to increase your chances of success make sure your goal is your goal, not your partner's, children's or society's.

The good, the bad and the ugly...
Get motivated by going through all the good stuff that happens when you achieve your goal, and all the bad stuff avoided. Bad stuff avoided is better – we take more action to avoid pain than to get pleasure. We'll come back to bad stuff.

Be accountable – it's you that's doing it and nobody cares about your pressures, childcare, lack of money or any other externality that you have chosen to blame in order to avoid the pain of discipline. Find a way. Overcome. Avoid regret.

Goal-directed action – is there another kind?
Know what your key activities are to achieve your goal and do them with maximum prejudice – anything or anyone who gets in your way will feel your wrath, unless you're sleeping with them, sired them, gave birth to them or they fit in some other extremely limited group, and even then.... remember you are the most important person in your life. That's not selfishness. It's the truth.

Now, the really bad stuff...
Jim Rohn, an American writer, said "we are destroyed from one of two pains; the pain of discipline or the pain of regret."

The pain of regret. I'm not sure I can think of anything worse. The massive, self-inflicted pain of regret. Yet we procrastinate. Why? Because the pain of discipline, although small, is here, right now. Whereas the pain of regret, although massive, is in the future.

But when you feel the pain of regret it is too late to do anything about it. And I don't think I could bear that. So I'm not going to.

In a Nutshell...
Motivation kills procrastination dead. Get motivated.

WHAT'S YOUR BIG SKILL? – 3 TESTS

I used to watch a man with an impressive title work a room full of clients. He could get round the room of fifty or so people in considerably less than an hour. He would approach a small group of people and stick out his hand, identify himself and say "what do you do?"

Great question. What do you do? The answers were usually job titles. I'm Director of Flimflammery. I'm Senior VP of Dissembling. I'm Declining Products Manager (this one is actually real, I promise you. Imagine his boss' reaction to a good sales year – "Now Jenkins, we've noticed that you've been selling rather a lot of Crapolene X5 this year. I hope you're not expecting a bonus...)

The really interesting question is not "what do you do?" It's "what are you really good at?" "What is your Big Skill?"

It takes some significant hard work to develop a Big Skill. Instead, it may be tempting to take the easy road - be jack-of-all trades. But Pollack was right when he said "life is hard if you live it the easy way and easy if you live it the hard way".

So what is your Big Skill, or what could it be?

When considering this question, there are three little tests to help you decide if your Big Skill is really big and, indeed, a skill. You don't need to get three out of three. I'd say the pass rate is nearer two out of three.

Here goes -

1. Your Big Skill gives you potential access to a wide range of markets.
Many people want your Big Skill. You are not limited to the Isle of Mull seaweed husbandry sector – you can deal with other islands and other plants.

2. Your Big Skill makes a major contribution to the perceived value of your products and services as seen by the customer.
Aahh...perceived value. One of my favourite couplets. Your Big Skill places you right at the heart of business – generating perceived value. The key word here is perceived. The customer sees it and values it. If they don't see what you thought was value (usually because they don't value it) then it isn't value.

Ask yourself this – "if I didn't exist, would the customer notice?"

3. Your Big Skill is not easily imitated by your competitors.
Your Big Skill takes a while to develop. It has breadth and depth. It is tangible and meaningful. Copying it is not easy and only the best could do it and most won't try.

How did you score?

In the work context, here's some Big Skills you may have -

Leading – generating a compelling and deliverable vision. Easier said than done. A Big Skill.

Managing – getting results through people. Simple as that. A Big Skill.

Marketing – finding people who are interested in your value and telling them about it. A Big Skill.

Intellectual property - maybe you have a database that allows you to generate insights for your clients, or you know the solution to a perennial problem, or you have some methodology that gets a great results, or you are an "expert"...all Big Skills.

Selling – closing deals. A Big Skill.

Operational excellence - making and delivering great products and services. A Big Skill.

All forms of **_development_** - R&D, Product/Service development etc – this is about meeting an unmet need. I put entrepreneurialism in this box. A Big Skill.

You may have one of these Big Skills on your business card but your business card is not you. So, remember the three tests: does your Big Skill...

Allow you access to lots of markets?

Deliver loads of perceived value?

And is it...

Difficult to copy?

Some of you may recognise the Big Skill as essentially being the Core Competency idea of Hamel and Prahalad, which is now about twenty years old. They applied it to the corporation. I think it is useful at a personal level as I've got this bizarre idea that corporations don't have skills, big or otherwise, but I think most people do.

In a Nutshell...
If your big skill doesn't pass these tests it isn't a big skill.

Do You Make Good Decisions?

We all make decisions all the time. And we are very rational. Are we not? We make rational decisions. This is called utility maximisation by economists. Economics is not called the dismal science for nothing you know.

This is how we make decisions: we look at all our options and we decide the relative likelihood of each actually occurring. Then we look at the value each option gives to us. We then synthesise this information and we make our choice. This is rational decision making.

However, what I have described is how a computer algorithm might make a decision. But we are not so clever. Or should I say not so rational.

We especially do not make decisions like a computer when there is a gain or a loss involved.

Two economists, Kahneman and Tversky won the Nobel Prize in 2002 for their work on what they called Prospect Theory, which describes decisions between alternatives where there is a risk involved.

Their studies showed that people are much more sensitive to a loss than to a gain. This is true to such an extent that people are willing to take on board serious risk to avoid a loss. For example, people sell shares when the stock market goes down, and they continue to pour money into something that they have put money into previously when they really should just walk away.

It was Warren Buffet who said that "losses gain twice the emotional response of gains."

People are risk-averse (i.e. they play it safe) in relation to gains, but are also loss-averse (and will gamble to avoid losses).

Makes no sense at all.

Here's an experiment – people were asked to imagine they were scientists and they were working on an outbreak of a nasty disease which was expected to kill 600 people. Two different programmes to fight the disease have been proposed. The first group of people were asked to decide between these two programmes –

A: 200 people will be saved.

B: there is a one third probability that 600 will be saved, and a two-thirds probability that no people will be saved.

In this case, 72% of the group favoured programme A.

A second group of people were asked to decide between these two programmes –

C: 400 people will die.

D: there is a one third probability that nobody will die, and a two thirds probability that 600 people will die.

Now you will see that A is the same as C and B is the same as D. It's just that the first choice (A or B) is *framed* as a choice between gains and the second choice (C or D) is framed as a choice between losses.

In the second case, 78% of people preferred programme D. Their preference has been reversed by changing the frame from gain to loss, although the options are essentially identical. Hmmm...

So, why care about this?

Well, marketers have us sussed and they use this to their advantage.

Would you rather get a 10% discount or avoid a 10% surcharge? It's the latter, because loss-avoidance trumps a gain. Hence the often used phrase "sign-up by the 17th or you will lose...", or "offer ends Sunday..."

Prospect theory explains both why we act when we shouldn't (usually to avoid loss, i.e. in selling shares when the market goes down) and why we don't act when we should. In fact, the more choices people have the more likely they are to do nothing. And the more good or attractive options there are, the worse the paralysis. And the longer the decision is deferred, the less likely it is that a decision will ever be made.

For example - one study asked people to complete a questionnaire for a decent reward: some were told the deadline was 5 days, others 21 days and a third group had no deadline. Results: 66% returned within the 5 day deadline, 40% in the 21 day deadline and 25% where there was no time limit. And it wasn't because they forgot.

So if you find yourself with decision paralysis, consider this –

Not to decide is itself a decision. Procrastination is a killer!

Think of opportunity cost, i.e. doing nothing may be more costly than doing something sub-optimal.

Play devil's advocate – challenge assumptions and consider the issue from scratch, not where you are today because what's already invested is a sunk cost. You cannot get it back no matter how much more love and money you throw at it.

In a Nutshell...
We are more emotionally wrapped up in loss than we are in gain. This can lead to poor decision making.

WHAT DRIVES YOUR DECISIONS – PAIN OR GAIN?

I've just thrown a book across the room. I will not finish it. It is obvious, superficial rubbish. I thought it would be better. I persevered. Really I did. I got almost half way through before it all became too much and I threw the book across the room. I felt faintly embarrassed, even although there was no one there.

This is the third book I have thrown across the room. I have read a lot of books. I should have thrown a lot more of them across the room. When I threw number two across the room about six months ago I promised myself that whenever I came across a book worthy of throwing across the room I would not hesitate. And I haven't. In future, I will throw a lot more books across the room.

What used to stop me throwing bad books across the room?
Well, when you buy a book and spent time reading it you are invested. Invested in the book. It would be a waste of money and time to stop reading it, wouldn't it?

Yes it would be a waste, but not of the book. It would be a waste of my time if I spent any more time reading a book I had developed a healthy hatred of. Spending more time reading will not make the book better or get me back the time I have already invested.

Taking conscious steps to create a loss is painful BUT essential
The book example is trivial. Books are cheap. But some of our investments are huge and walking away from them is very painful. But I would argue that if the investment is no longer giving you the return you need, it's time to stop investing. If you can get some of what you have invested back that's great but if you can't that shouldn't change the decision to walk.

Some examples –

- **Relationships** – are you getting what you signed up for? Still waiting for things to get better? Don't wait too long.

- **Job** – thrilled to be Head of Department. Good for you. But when it stops turning you on and you know you're not just going through a sticky patch...get your coat on.

- **Beliefs** – there's a lot of physicists right now girding their loins, hoping they don't have to accept that some particles CAN go faster than the speed of light. It's difficult to walk away from something that you have believed for decades.

- **Money** - your investment halved in value? Sell it before there's nothing left.

- **Identity** – I am a research scientist and I do research science. Hmm...maybe. Beware expertise – it's often a rut.

All of these invested positions cause *standstill* – an inability to take action because we feel walking away from what we have invested so much in is simply too painful.

You may also know this phenomenon as "sunk costs" – the investment has been made, you cannot get it all back. Continuing to invest more money hoping that the prior investment will turn around makes no sense. Ten pounds spent today does not increase the value of ten pounds spent yesterday.

We are wired to avoid pain but decision making based on avoiding pain rather than achieving gain gives poor results.

Trying to achieve gain is almost always the better decision. It is almost always better to move than to stand still.

It seems that the aphorism really is true: "no pain, no gain"
Once again, our pre-historic brain-wiring does not help us in the post-sabre-toothed-tiger age. But our awareness will save us – so let's make sure that we regularly ask ourselves if we are making decisions based on avoiding loss or on attracting gain.

And when a book needs throwing, throw it.

Dr Mark J Nugent

In a Nutshell...

Ride your winners and cut your losses - in all walks of life. Most of us fail to cut our losses. This is wrong because they just mount up.

SELF-CONFIDENCE REVISITED

It's been only a few short months since I wrote of Self-Confidence and I'm being asked about it again. Despite us living here in one of the richest countries on earth, with 90% of the world's population willing to swap places with us at the drop of a hat, this remains a huge issue.

My soufflé won't rise...
Self-confidence cannot simply be summoned up by your brain. Positive thinking only gets you so far. You are unlikely to become the world's best soufflé chef by thinking about it.

We are all in sales...
You are unlikely to be a confident, self-assured small business person if the only thing you're good at is your product, what you deliver. Not if you have other responsibilities, like sales and sales and sales.

Blockers...
Without doubt there are blockers to self-confidence –

* All dependencies – whether people, drugs, habits or beliefs.

* All comparisons – of yourself with others.

* Don't repress your desires, they will never go away. The act of repression implies that you feel the desire is bad and then you are bad.

Would the real barrier please stand up...
But the real blocker is poor competence or skill. Self-confidence is an output. It's not an input. You become self-confident when you purposely set out to become skilled and capable at a task. In time, when you hone your skills, it will come. Sporadic bouts of activity, driven largely out of fear and desperation, like the sales guy who hates making calls then makes 100 in a day, and then none for the next two weeks – this compounds and ingrains poor self-confidence. Vicious cycle.

You don't start with...
...self-confidence. You end with self-confidence.

Of course once competent your self-confidence will increase and this will spill over to become part of your demeanour and will make the attainment of self-confidence in other areas of your life easier. Virtuous cycle.

So what to do...
Think of the one area where supreme self-confidence would change your life. I mean really change it. Be specific. Plan to do this thing – put it in your diary. Make a promise to yourself. Now plan for this event. Once you've done it, review how it went. Seek feedback. Now plan again for the next time. Then do it. Then review.
Plan-Do-Review-Plan-Do-Review....they call it continuous improvement.

Take your medicine...
I cannot stress enough that the one great medicine, the cure-all, that almost always works in almost all situations, that makes you feel better mentally and physically, that generates what those that don't take the medicine call "luck"...is...ACTION.

Just do it. Self-confidence is an output. It will come.

In a Nutshell...
Self-confidence is a result of action. Don't wait for it to appear, create it.

Conditioning

How to stop your elephant running away? Easy – tie one foot to a small stake in the ground. The elephant can easily pull the stake out. But it doesn't. Why? Because when it was young, the elephant was tied to a stake it couldn't pull out of the ground. It would pull, and pull and pull. To no avail. The baby elephant became **conditioned**. The truth was that the elephant simply could not uproot the stake. Now the elephant weights five tons and is ten feet high and it can easily pull up the stake. But it doesn't. The elephant has a firm view of what it can and cannot do. And it knows it cannot uproot the stake, even although it really can. The barrier is in the elephant's head.

Some people are **conditioned** in the same way. They are like the elephant – they know what they cannot do and they are right. This conditioning comes from our families – "don't bite off more than you can chew". Well meaning, but limiting. Conditioning also comes from society – the huge pressure to conform. This leads directly to mediocrity. Then there are mistakes and failures – we are told these are bad, so we get embarrassed and the famous fear of failure is born. Failure itself is unimportant. Our attitude towards it is crucial. And our attitude is a choice.

How to break out of this? First – self-knowledge. Examine our habits, values and the things we believe in. Become aware of our strengths and our weaknesses. Decide what to change. Then set goals (of course) – to organise and direct our daily activity and make the best use of our potential. Finally - develop new attitudes and habits – the ones we want and need to deliver our goals.

Turn the tables on conditioning – let's condition ourselves. Pull the stake out the ground! As Nehru said at the top, the way you play your cards is free will.

In a Nutshell...
Your conditioning is likely to limit you.

LIZARD BRAIN VS. IBRAIN

I am a keen observer of human behaviour, particularly my own. It's not always pretty, but I try to keep it behind closed doors. I went cycling on Saturday – new target – 25 miles. I procrastinated for 10 minutes before I actually got on the bike. I always do. I get my gear on and then...I don't walk out the door. I mess around for ten or fifteen minutes. I know I *will* walk out the door – I never give in and decide not to cycle – that would be too horrible to deal with. I always go out, but I do delay the actual departure.

I find something to do – on Saturday it was making sure Match of the Day is set to record; checking the route again on Google maps; having a quick espresso – all classics of the art of procrastination. I could write a book.

Cold blooded...
So why do I do this? Well, there's a part of my brain that was designed a long, long time ago in a swamp somewhere in a country with no name and the software that runs that part of my brain has not been updated...ever. Let's call it my lizard brain. And my lizard brain only does two things – it seeks pleasure and it avoids pain. And it much prefers the latter because you cannot do the former if you're dead.

Oh the pain...
And my lizard brain hates the first two miles of the bike ride. Because it's hard. It's the hardest two miles of the whole ride. So there's a bit of pain and my lizard brain wants to avoid pain. So I procrastinate for 10 minutes, pointlessly.

Introducing iBrain...
The avoidance of pain is actually very powerful and my software updated present day brain (let's call it the iBrain – you heard it here first) can use this to great effect. The trick is this – you need to find the bigger pain, the future pain. What's the pain associated with not going out on the bike; making that presentation; asking for the raise; saying goodbye? When my iBrain identifies the bigger, future pain and

tries to avoid that pain, rather than the smaller today pain favoured by the lizard brain, then we overcome procrastination.

I do think this is one of the real keys to self-management. To put the lizard back in its box. The reason we do not do what we need to do is because we focus on the wrong pain – the small, immediate pain. But if we get our iBrain to focus on the big, future pain and its desire to avoid that pain, then the small immediate pain is just something to get through. It's a simple discipline issue.

Get some perspective...
The problem with the small immediate pain is that it's two inches in front of our nose and therefore it seems bigger than the large future pain. Or even worse, it blocks out all sight of the big future pain and we just cannot see what's coming should we shrink before the smaller pain.

So, although my pre-cycle procrastination is hardly the worse thing in the world, it's still useless and reptilian so today when the time comes I shall engage iBrain and put my gear on and walk straight out the door and ten minutes later the small today pain will be behind me and the lizard will be back in his box.

In a Nutshell...
Avoiding the pain today is why we procrastinate. Avoiding the bigger pain of tomorrow is why we mustn't procrastinate.

THINK YOU'RE PROACTIVE? - TAKE MY TEST

How proactive are we really? It's an interesting question.

The answer is not as proactive as we think – which is a relief otherwise I'd have nothing to write about this week.

I think we are designed to go with the flow. It takes massive action to break out of this, but break out of it we must. But only the few will make it. You may be one of them.

It's so easy to switch off. To let the autopilot define the destination. To let the alarm clock wake us up; to eat the same breakfast; to react the same way to the same stimuli – boss, partner, issues, problems, opportunities; to think the same thoughts. To be catalysed into action by external events – the email, the phone, work colleagues. To fail to take charge.

I really challenged myself on this last week. I secretly wondered if I was just getting up and doing the same things not because they were the right things but because they were the things I do.

So, being a big fan of tests with easy questions (and difficult answers) I made up a test for myself. I have called it Mark's Proactivity Tester. Pretty snappy I think you'll agree?

Now, I understand that some of the questions may not be relevant to you. For example, if your job is to pick up the phone before it rings three times you may struggle with question no 2. So if your job makes you do crazy things, don't pay too much attention to the questions that show that fact up!

So here it is...

Ask yourself these questions...

1. When I get an email, I...

a) Read it.

b) Don't read it.

c) Don't know I've received an email.

2. When the phone rings, I...

a) Answer it.

b) Don't answer it.

c) Don't know I've received a phone call.

3. When someone says "do you have a minute", I reply...

a) "Of course, shall we get some tea?"

b) "If it's a quickie" (ooh-err Missus)

c) "I'm just working on something right now; can you come back at 2 o'clock?"

4. When I am working on something, I...

a) Constantly interrupt myself to do other things.

b) Repeatedly think about the next thing on my list.

c) Focus on what I'm doing to a very high degree, and I'm not really sure what's next on my list but that's OK because I have a system where everything is under control.

5. I feel as if I am in charge of my destiny (the key word is destiny – this is not about being in charge of every minute of every day – no one has that luxury)...

a) Pretty much never.

b) Sometimes.

c) Pretty much always.

6. My goals are...

a) Given to me.

b) Negotiated by me.

c) Defined by me.

7. The purpose of my life is...

a) You're not catching me out with that mumbo-jumbo...purpose! Ha!

b) A work in progress.

c) Clear to me.

8. I have a written list of high-payoff activities...

a) You're joking; I don't even have goals.

b) In my head, honest, trust me.

c) In my diary.

9. The stuff in my diary this week makes me feel...

a) Nauseous.

b) OK – just another week.

c) Like it's another step in the right direction.

OK there's no scoring system here but if you've had sufficient coffee today you will have realised that answering c) is better than b) is better than a).

So take a view

We are all somewhere on the reactivity/proactivity line. For me the target is total proactivity. This won't happen but it's a target worth striving for. Because total proactivity equals total freedom and I like the sound of that. So I'm going to keep asking myself these nine questions...just to be on the safe side.

In a Nutshell...

We can be reactive or proactive. Proactivity takes effort, and therefore is a conscious choice. If you don't choose it, reactivity is the default.

GETTING SOME HELP

I have an accountant for my accounts, a golfer for my golf swing, an investor for my investments, a trader for my trades and my wife to tell me where I'm going wrong...

They all help, in their way...
Some have hard skills; some soft. But they all help.

But more than this...
I have Drayton Bird to help me with marketing. I have Michael Porter to help me with strategy. I have a man to help me with changing my business model. I have another to help me with internet marketing. I have Mr X to coach me (that's not his real name – that would be weird).

There are literally dozens more. Dozens. I pay all of these people, one way or another. Some I have never met, but they still help me.

I have no ego...
Not when it comes to seeking help. Help with my business. And with managing me. Anyone who spends their time re-inventing wheels is nuts.

This is a call-to-action. Get some help.

You may think...
...this Pearl is self-serving. That I am touting for business. I'm not. I actually believe this stuff. If you're not convinced, ask yourself this as you try to re-invent the wheel: as a manager grows and becomes more successful, do you think he or she, in general, makes more or less use of coaches and mentors?

It's more. Fact.

I have spent...

...many thousands of pounds of my own money in the last year alone on coaches and mentors. I'd like to spend more. The return on investment will be at least 50 times the spend and possibly a lot more. But it's up to me to take the massive action required. I am and will.

Ask a professional athlete to imagine life without a coach. They will look at you as if you are stupid.

They cannot imagine it.

A teacher – someone who shows you how to do something. They have a skill to impart to you.

A coach – someone to help you realise your potential. They may not be better at the activity than you, but that's not the point.

A mentor – someone who has done what you want to do and can show you the way. Like satnav for your aspiration.

Some people think asking for help is a sign of failure. No. Not asking is a guarantor of failure. People will read a manual on how to work the telly, but they won't read a manual on how to run their business, or themselves.

Any colour, as long as it's black...

Even if you do reinvent that wheel, and it doesn't take too long, you still have to re-invent the engine, and the tyres, and everything else. And once you've done all that, you have something that looks like a crap version of Henry Ford's 1896 classic Quadracycle. But we're living in the 21st Century.

Get some help.

In a Nutshell...

Saving money by not buying help to speed business and personal improvement whilst spending time to work out what's already known to others is a common affliction of the less successful business person.

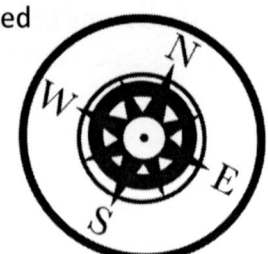

MY OBSERVATIONS OF SUCCESSFUL PEOPLE

There are a lot of trees sacrificed in the production of books by high profile successful people purporting to tell you how they achieved it all. I find the problem with a lot of this genre is that the authors assume that EVERYTHING they did contributed to their success. So you end up with people saying nonsense like you must eat raw broccoli in the morning or you must speak to at least one customer every single day...

Of course it's all very specific to the individual and as such of no real coaching value. So I thought I'd have a wee think about the successful people I've known and know still.

In my corporate life I had met a lot of people who would consider themselves successful. In the more recent coaching years, I have met a lot more, and from a much more diverse collection of jobs, industries and cultures.

A lot of these people are really successful. By successful I mean that at any given point they know what their "desired future state" looks like and they are making good progress towards it. The future state can, of course, be anything you like. Success has many forms.

I've been thinking about what characterises these people. I have constructed a short list of ten. The list is not comprehensive – there are other characteristics not mentioned. And it is not a blueprint – some of the successful people I am thinking of have characteristics opposite to those listed. But most of the success people exhibit most of the characteristics.

Here goes -

1. They are relentlessly positive
Not head-in-the-sand-positive, but the positive that comes from having a goal, taking action, getting results, moving in the right direction and understanding that there is no failure, only results.

2. They focus on their talents
They understand that by doing this they stand a much greater chance of making progress. The alternative – ignoring talents and trying to correct weaknesses is a mug's game. I'm glad Plato did what he did instead of obsessing about his shyness.

3. They work, work, work
Talents are raw materials. But it is work that turns them into strengths. Without the work we have what is known as "wasted talent". You often find in sports that the most successful have the most talent AND the highest work ethic. It's an intoxicating brew.

4. They are inquisitive and love to learn
To successful people, nothing stands still, including their own world view. They educate themselves constantly. And this also makes them humble because they are constantly reminded of what they don't know.

5. They think big
They understand that most barriers are in the head. They ask themselves "and how could we do ten times more." They don't let a lack of something get in the way. They simply add it's acquisition to their To Do List.

6. They are highly productive
They understand what needs to be done and what's just fluff. They spend a lot of time on the important stuff, in blocks of time, and they deal effectively with the rest. They have LARGE wastepaper bins that are well used.

7. They have lots of time off
They know when the next holiday is. They often work in quite intense blocks of up to ten weeks (weekends off of course) and then have a holiday to refresh. Work hard, play hard – repeat to fade.

8. If they are men and married with children, their wives tend to look after the children rather than work
I was surprised by this but there it is.

9. They help others to grow
They delegate thoughtfully. They coach others. They see life as a win-win, not a zero-sum game.

10. They are happy
They usually have a twinkle in their eye and a laugh is never far away.

All of these characteristics, and particularly the last one, are all predicated on the people being successful by THEIR definition, not someone else's. There lies madness.

In a Nutshell...
Most successful people exhibit most of these characteristics. You can model them.

How Biased Are You?

It's a wonder we ever get anything right.

Cognitive bias is a fancy-pants name for all the "distortions in the human mind that are hard to avoid and lead to perceptions and judgements that deviate from the reality..." – Rudiger and Pohl in "Cognitive Illusions". I haven't read it.

And all this happens involuntarily and without our knowledge.

Jeeze. That explains a few things...

Hindsight Bias...the inclination to see past events as predictable.

Yup – got that one.

Fundamental Attribution Error...basically – "he did bad stuff because he's bad", not because he was in a bad situation (and maybe had been for a very long time).

I'm OK on this one I think.

Rationalisation...constructing a logical justification for an emotional decision.

Used to do this. Not anymore. I now know I am much, much more emotional than I ever thought. Just kept a lid on it.

Bandwagon Effect...the tendency to do or believe something because others do.

Ha! Don't have any of this...or do I? Hmmm. The casual observer may disagree.

Confirmation Bias...a classic. Searching for evidence to back up your case, rather than gathering all the evidence and taking a balanced view.

Got this one licked usually, unless I'm clearly right in which case I'm not biased am I?

Status Quo Bias...the preference towards alternatives that maintain the current situation.

Alternative Vote system anyone? I'll be voting yes. Anarchy in the UK!

Illusion of control...the tendency for human beings to believe they can control outcomes when they cannot.

Messed up big on this one once when v young. Cost my employer a bob or too. Still, we all learned from it!

Recallability Trap...giving great weight to recent events over past events.

The M1 is shut just now because there was a fire in a scrap yard near to the carriageway. I heard some politician calling for specific new legislation to stop scrap yards going on fire. I laughed out loud while chopping a shallot. Almost cut my bloody hand off. The boys said "what is it Daddy?" I couldn't begin to explain.

Sunk Cost Bias...another classic. To make decisions in a way that justifies past decisions, even if they are no longer relevant.

I know someone who will not throw stuff out because at that point it becomes "a waste". No, if you don't use it and it's lying around, it's already a waste. I'm not telling you who this person is. I don't think she reads my blog. Why would she?

Loss Aversion...tendency to strongly prefer avoiding losses to making gains.

Here's a question for you. You buy a share in company A for £10 and one in company B for £10. Two weeks later the A share is at £5 and the B share is at £15. What do you do? –

a) sell both

b) keep both

c) sell A and keep B

d) keep A and sell B

Answer at the bottom.

Anchoring...when making a decision, the mind gives too much weight to the first information received.

Yes....I never liked him from the moment I met him. Oops.

Survivorship Bias....failure to include "deaths" in your research, e.g. when doing market research failing to include in the sample those who no longer buy, or got close but swerved at the last minute.

Goodness me we are frail beings are we not? All these biases to overcome. The brain really is amazing, but, as I've said before, it's not user-friendly and has no manual. Still, forewarned is forearmed, as they say.

ANSWER

c) sell A and keep B.

Cut your losses and ride your winners. Most people would keep A and wait for it to "come good". They would also sell B to realise a small gain. The likelihood is that A will continue to decline and B will continue to rise, so selling A to prevent further losses and holding B to realise greater gains is the correct answer, usually. But loss aversion prevents us from doing the right thing.

In a Nutshell...

We have a natural tendency towards bias. This leads to poor decision making.

MORAL HAZARD

I am just back from RIAT - The Royal International Air Tattoo at Fairford in rural Gloucestershire. I went with my boys, 9 and 6. That's not their names. This is our 5th year. There's a show on Saturday and Sunday. This year we decided to go on both days. It was great.

There are 80,000 visitors per day. It's a great environment for kids - basically no cars. It's a playground 2 miles long and 400 yards wide.

If you lose your kids they will be safe. But how do you find them?

They have a system - when you arrive you get a wristband for the kids with your mobile number on it. We have used this system every year. We have yet to lose our kids, but they have often strayed and have alluded to the wristband as their insurance policy. They allow themselves a wide perimeter - 30 or 40 feet, but that's plenty to get lost in in a crowd of 80,000 people.

This was stressful for my wife and me. It took constant supervision and the children clearly felt no risk. My wife couldn't come this year - had to deal with her late father's estate.

So it was me and two kids, for two days, in a huge playground with 80,000 people. Hmmmmm. I am feeling outnumbered. Time for new tactics.

Me and the boys walked through the gate on Saturday morning. The nice man with the single tooth in the middle of his upper gum (really) informed me about the wristband system but I declined.

Boy1 said "what if we get lost." I said "well then, you're lost." Boy2 stared at me. That's not their names either.

The kids were shocked.

What happened?

Dr Mark J Nugent

The boys never strayed more than 15 feet from me at any time during the entire two days. They weren't fearful; they had simply moved their locus of security from a wristband to their father. They had a great time. Boy1 declared it the best airshow ever. Boy2 agreed through a mouthful of chips.

The wristband is a safety net. I guess safety nets serve a purpose. But if they change behaviour, as the wristband system had done with my boys on previous years, then maybe they are not really a safety net. (The marshalling yard for lost wristband wearers was mobbed with tearful kids at kicking out time - maybe their parents couldn't get a mobile signal, as I couldn't. It is rural Gloucestershire after all.)

I guess the question is - do you have any safety nets that change your behaviours and if so, is it a change for the better?

In a Nutshell...
Safety nets can increase risk taking. This is dangerous.

Do You Focus on Strengths or Weaknesses?

I think it was Winston Churchill who said "I am easily satisfied with the very best". I wonder if we always strive to deliver the very best to our clients. I wonder. Because to do so requires an unbelievable laser-like focus on their fears and frustrations, needs and desires, to the exclusion of all else.

I recently have experienced two offerings that are truly excellent – world class, honed, magnificent, near perfect.

C'est Magnifique...
The first was an overnight stay with dinner and breakfast at Raymond Blanc's Le Manoir Aux Quat'Saisons in Great Milton. I won't go into the minutiae of what it was like to stay in a 2 Michelin star Oxfordshire country pile but suffice to say they know what they're doing and they do it superbly and have been for 25 years. Right down to the perfect lemon cake with afternoon tea. And they make money.

Fruity...
The second magnificent experience is Blackberry. In October last year I changed my Blackberry for an HTC smartphone. Once my initial ardour had subsided I was left with something that, although brilliant for some, was not brilliant for me. Despite the massive capability of the thing, it couldn't do well what I needed – to call the right number when I needed it to without having to push 8 buttons, and to send, receive and manage emails and texts efficiently and effectively. I got to the stage where I was scared to pick it up because to do so invariably activated some App, or called the wrong person.

So, I went back to Blackberry and was reminded all over again how their product, for me, is world class, honed, magnificent, near perfect. And they make money.

School's out...
The reason I question whether we aim to be excellent is because we are taught to be average. Having just had parent's *evening* for my two

boys (held from 4 to 6pm – eh...don't get me started) I am struck once again by the focus on "failure" – the areas where the child is excellent are "banked", with relief, and the focus turns to the "weaknesses" in an attempt to get them to the average. Now don't get me wrong, the basics must be secured at a minimum level – reading, writing and arithmetic. That's fine. But once this has been achieved, the focus should be on excellence – focus on strengths, not weaknesses, whether it be academic, vocational, sport, art etc.

Role models...
Every business biography I read – the leaders in question focused on their strengths and managed their weaknesses – usually by getting someone else to do it.

Free transfer...
And in sport – do top sports teams try to get their under-performers up to snuff? No. They let them go and they focus on making the great ones superstars. A focus on excellence.

Business is not about being perfect. In business, value = money.

VALUE = MONEY...

The more value you give, the more money you will attract. At a high level, it's a true differentiator and of course it fits with the well-honed idea that there's only two business strategies – niche or massive. Le Manoir or MacDonald's. Each is valid but for the small business person where customer intimacy is often key; the customer will be disappointed if you put a burger down in front of them.

So, for all of you who have "tart up the website", "rewrite the brochure", "redesign the logo" etc. on your to-do list today – score them out, now. Ask yourself what fears, frustrations, hopes and desires you fulfil for your clients and how can you do more of this and do it better. A relentless focus on this will make your business even better than it is and maybe one day some idiot will be blogging about your lemon cake and in so doing generate more custom for you.

In a Nutshell...
Winners focus on their strengths.

WHAT I LEARNED IN 2009

I have been working for others and now myself for a total of 21 years and 2 months. Reflection is something I am not sure I am terribly good at, not because I cannot do it, but I tend to devote insufficient time to it, due to being excessively future-focused. So I've been trying to make amends. I have been reflecting. Here are some conclusions. Apologies to those whose well-honed words I have mangled.

1. I believe the greatest thing ever is the human being.
2. I believe that the greatest time to be alive is right now.
3. I believe the greatest waste on earth is human potential.
4. I believe formal education does half the job it should.
5. I believe that intelligence as we perceive it is a poor proxy for ability.
6. I believe attitude is all.
7. I believe that attitude is a choice.
8. I believe that it is not ignorance that will kill me, but what I think to be true that is, in fact, false.
9. I believe integrity is measured by what I do when no one's looking.
10. I believe that I shouldn't do anything unless I am prepared to describe fully my motivations and desires to a child.
11. I believe that most people can achieve anything they want but most will not dare try.
12. I believe that having hand-written goals is an absolute pre-requisite to my achievement.
13. I believe I must have my own plan otherwise I am doomed to be part of someone else's plan.
14. I believe that some of my old relationships are bad for at least one of the parties involved.
15. I believe that until I master marketing, I run the risk of being a busy fool.
16. I believe the internet offers the greatest opportunity to my and most other small businesses, including those who will never

sell anything through it.

17. I believe that self-management and self-leadership must come first for me.

18. I believe I have more control over myself than over anything else and I should act accordingly.

19. I believe I will leave most of my potential on the table if I don't have a coach and mentor.

20. I believe that personal development is my duty to myself.

21. I believe that most people will spend more in a year on cafe lattes than on personal development.

22. I believe that true leaders are humble, largely because they constantly educate themselves, and this is a reminder of how little they know.

23. I believe people always do the best they can, although sometimes their best disappoints.

24. I believe satisfaction lasts longer than happiness.

25. I believe I cannot motivate anyone.

26. I believe I can inspire.

27. I believe that too many people "settle" for what's "OK" and then lie to themselves.

28. I believe discipline hurts less than regret.

29. I believe that singing is better than dying with the song still in me.

30. I believe that 2010 will be your best ever year. You can do it.

In a Nutshell...

A small amount of time spent reflecting is time well spent.

What I Learned In 2010

As 2010 draws to a snowy close I reflect on the completion of my third year in business and I ask myself "What have I learned?"

Quite a lot really...
There is abundant opportunity...

I never really "got" this. But now I do. Life really isn't a zero sum game at any level. It's just that sometimes it can seem that way if we set low goals and miss them, do the wrong things, fail to do enough of the right things, target the wrong markets, and go about our business fearfully and defensively. Then it's a struggle.

But with clarity, focus, confidence, real personal productivity and a laser-like focus on what we need, it comes to us, once we know what it looks like.

We've got to love what we do...
This is about values. If we spend huge amounts of time doing stuff that doesn't accord tightly with our values we're running on the wrong fuel. Values drive behaviour and behaviour drives results.

I finally realised my one core value that isn't banal is that I believe the greatest thing on earth is human potential and I will do what I can do make sure more of it is realised. This has been hugely clarifying for me. I guess I kind of knew it, but sitting down in a darkened room and homing in on my one core value has really helped me. I now do more of the right stuff and I have cut out a lot of the stuff that was not value-driven. Relief! It's like being let out of jail.

We have everything we need...
It's all here. Centuries of human endeavour, experience, knowledge. And all the people around us right now. Here's a great question to ask someone. It gets a positive and valuable response 95 times out of a hundred. "Can you help me with......?" Try it.

If you boil a kettle it boils at a hundred degrees. Every time. If you do the things that people have done before you will get their results. This is not weird. It would be weird if it was not so.

The past is gone...

Good and bad. To relive it is a choice. Not a destiny. We are all conditioned to an almost frightening extent. But the conditioning process is not over. We are alive to conditioning now...right now. And we can do it to ourselves. And it doesn't take long. Some people say 21 days to recondition ourselves in any area. I think that's about right.

Our future is unwritten...

But it will be written. We can write it. We should write it. Because if we don't someone else will. If we don't have our own plan, we will be a part of someone else's plan. Stark choice.

Our brain is beyond fantastic...

But it isn't user friendly and it doesn't come with a manual. We need to manage ourselves first and foremost, before we try to manage anything else. Deal with fear. Change the level of fear attributed to an action. As Jim Rohn said "we are destined to suffer from one of two pains – the pain of discipline or the pain of regret." Learn to fear regret with a vengeance. As a child fears monsters. Then the fear of discipline seems trivial. And procrastination and all the other stuff that hold us back are revealed to be just mice wearing monster suits.

We need to stop and reflect...

I am amazed at how the people I consider to be successful switch off all the screens and take the time out to reflect on what they've done, to plan, to spend really good time with their families and come back renewed, refreshed, sharper than before, ready for the next chapter.

In a Nutshell...
We have all we need.

WHAT I LEARNED IN 2011

That's my fourth year of self-employment chalked up. I have had ups and downs but I am more confident today about the future than I have ever been. The potential is massive and fortune favours the brave.

As always, I ask myself what I have learned. I never did this in corporate life. But I'm not in corporate life any more. I'm in life. And this stuff matters.

So, what have I learned?

1. The Playing Field Has Never Been More Level
The internet, coupled with cheap, powerful online services have levelled the playing field for a lot of small business owners in terms of product delivery and marketing.

You can get a simple website up in a matter of hours. You can automate a sales cycle in an hour. You can print on demand a single copy of a 250 page book and ship it anywhere on earth for less than ten US dollars. You can use simple and cheap tools to attract potential customers.

All of this capability was until very recently either impossible or very expensive. This tilted the game in favour of large, established corporations. No longer. You can kill giants.

2. Interruption Marketing is Dead or Dying
All unrequested marketing – TV ads, junk mail, flyers, telesales etc. is either dead or dying. It is expensive and ineffective. This is also known as push or outbound marketing.

Inbound marketing is the future. I give my stuff away for nothing and those who are interested follow me. I use permission-based marketing to offer my prospects products and services. I sell to those who are interested, not the mass. And it doesn't feel like selling.

3. I Need a Mentor and a Coach
A mentor = someone who has done what I plan to do.

My *mentor* builds my confidence and shortens my journey. Re-inventing the wheel is just stupid.

A *coach* – someone who helps me to reach my potential.

It's difficult to keep on keeping on by yourself. Most MegaCorp directors have a coach. ALL sports people have a coach.

They are worth their weight in gold.

4. Invest in Education
I have spent thousands of pounds on my own education in the last three years. I am learning now at a faster rate than at any time in my life.

Everything I need to get everything I want is already known. I go and get it. I learn it.

The payback on this investment is astronomical.

5. Rituals Are Powerful
My morning ritual, or practice, is incredibly powerful. It focuses me, calms me and fills me with confidence. It is not a habit. Habits are mindless and robotic. But a ritual or a practice is conscious and can be continuously improved.

6. Worship GOYA
Not the Spanish Romantic painter, but **Get Off Your Arse.**

I take massive action. I have a bias towards action. I take the first step; even if I cannot see the other steps, I only need to see the first one. I take it. I trust that things will work out. Action is almost always better than inaction.

With action I get a result which I can analyse and make a change to my next action. And so it goes on.

With sitting on my arse I just get a bigger arse.

7. Blocktime is Essential

I cannot build Rome in sixty minute chunks between meetings. When I am creating something significant or making a change in my business (like moving from a *my-time-your-money* model to a *getting-paid-without-turning-up* model) I recognise this as a strategic issue and give it blocks of time. I'm talking days or even weeks dedicated to a task.

8. I Really, Actually, Truly, Have Nothing to Lose

As I wrote recently, Steve Jobs said, before he knew of his cancer, that we are all going to die *so what is it you are afraid of losing*?

I am going to lose it all anyway. I might as well just jump in.

9. Like a Horror Movie: My Fear of X Delivers X in Abundance

My fear of failure delivers failure to me.

My fear of rejection delivers rejection to me.

My fear of pain delivers pain to me.

I try to be fearless. It is not always easy. But I remember that this type of "in the head" fear is an artefact of my lizard brain — the old and first part of my brain that is constantly on the lookout for something to be frightened of. And if my lizard brain cannot find a hungry lion to be frightened of it will focus instead on that difficult phone call I have to make and treat that as the hungry lion. Crazy but true. My lizard brain just wants to keep me safe. But, like an over-protective mother, she can smother me. I stay aware of this.

10. I Am My Psychology

The tools and techniques of management and leadership are necessary for success. They are freely or inexpensively available to me.

They are necessary but insufficient. They are only half the game.

The other half is my psychology. My mindset of success. This is not taught in schools or universities. It is poorly taught if at all in corporations. It is well understood by some elite sports people.

Every single day I see and hear people who inadvertently reveal an aspect of their psychology that is severely limiting them.

And they are oblivious to their limitation. Presumably because it isn't tangible. What a waste.

I don't even have to master my psychology, although I am trying to. Simple awareness of the elements of my psychology and how they can either help or hinder me is half the battle. I then make sure that any unhelpful stuff is snuffed out pretty quickly. That does the rest of the job.

Tools, techniques AND positive psychology – the only winning combination I need and the only winning combination there has ever been.

In a Nutshell...
The plan-do-review cycle works. The review part should be little and often – maybe monthly or quarterly. But take the time to do it properly once per year.

INDEX

Lightning Source UK Ltd.
Milton Keynes UK
UKOW031835260512

193373UK00001B/1/P